NAOMI

AND THE

WIDOWS' CLUB

A Safe Strong Place after the Loss of a Spouse

NAOMI RHODE
& KIM HARMS

with
Lynda Hislop, Kathy Dempsey, Beth Klement, Luan Jackson,
Marylen Veden, Pam Bennett and Judy Huber

Naomi and the Widows' Club: A Safe Strong Place After The Loss Of A Spouse

Printed in the United States of America

Hardcover ISBN: 978-1-958714-61-4
Paperback ISBN: 978-1-958714-62-1
Ebook ISBN: 978-1-958714-63-8

Library of Congress Control Number: 2022950712

Muse Literary
3319 N. Cicero Avenue
Chicago IL 60641-9998

The Welcoming Prayer by Father Thomas Keating was used with permission of Contemplative Outreach and taken from their website.
All Biblical References from the New International Version of the Bible unless otherwise noted. The King James version is also used and, when used, noted.

Scriptures are taken from the Holy Bible, New International Version®, NIV®. Copyright © 1973, 1978, 1984, 2011 by Biblica, Inc.™ Used by permission of Zondervan. All rights reserved worldwide. www.zondervan. com The "NIV" and "New International Version" are trademarks registered in the United States Patent and Trademark Office by Biblica, Inc.™

What People are Saying

"Widows need and deserve love. Naomi and friends have created a must-read book for every widow and friend of a widow. Their grief is real. Until now, no one has addressed this important subject skillfully with insiders' wisdom, love, compassion, and deep experience. I believe this book will do for widowhood what Dr. Elisabeth Kubler Ross' book did for Death and Dying."

—Mark Victor Hansen, co-creator of *Chicken Soup for the Soul* and *ASK* series

"Naomi Rhode and her friends have given us a gift in their new book. Remember it was James who reminded us that 'pure religion' was to visit orphans and the widows. We, as a church, have not done well in focusing on this obvious command of scripture to care for the widows among us. It appeared to be a priority in the early church (Acts 6:1). There are times we wonder if we are pleasing the Lord with our endeavors. Rhode and her widows guide us to the heart of God on this truth of compassion."

—Dr. Darryl DelHousaye, Pastor Emeritus, Scottsdale Bible Church, Chancellor of Phoenix Seminary

"I'm convinced this book can be a great healer to widows feeling the emptiness of the loss of their spouses. That enormous void can be filled with God's love and the grace and comfort only found in the arms of Jesus."

—Captain Charlie Plumb, Former POW, Keynote Speaker, Seminar Leader

"Naomi and the Widows' Club: A Safe Strong Place after the Loss of a Spouse is a beautifully written tapestry on loss and grief weaved together by the authors Naomi Rhode, and the eight widows who have encountered the death of their spouse.

As I read this poignant book, each story was a touchpoint of remembrance for my own feelings and emotions after the death of my spouse and was a soothing balm of hope and encouragement.

Throughout the chapters, Naomi tenderly weaves the spectrum of other losses in our lives—a major move, the loss of a place, a home, health, and relationships—to include women who face a different grief.

This must-read book offers a theme related to loss for each chapter, with encouraging scripture, heart-felt questions to ponder, and comforting prayers. *Naomi and the Widows' Club* is ideally suited for small group or individual study."

—Susan Miller, Executive Director & Founder, Just Moved Ministry

"I read *Naomi and the Widows' Club* through two lenses of experience. As an adult learning theorist who has advised on bereavement research, I recognize the deep interpersonal connections between these women that are vital to their shared journey beyond the healing of loss to horizons of new becoming. They are traversing this courageous journey of renewal arm-in-arm with one another and their ever-present God who is their safe strong place. Their stories have blessed me with new insights I wish I could have accessed long ago as a young 32-year-old widow and single parent. If I could step back in time with these new insights, I would search far and wide for what God has created through *Naomi and the Widows' Club*. And if it could not be found, I would do as these women have done and dare to create it!

—Debra A. Fisher, Ph.D., MS Ed, President/Owner, CastleBridge Research Consulting

"Widows occupy a special place in the heart of God. This book uses deep stories to minister in a profound way to widows everywhere. You will be blessed."

—Michael Farris, President and CEO, Alliance Defending Freedom

"I'm so grateful that Naomi followed God's prompting to bring together not just a group of widows she could encourage, but also a book for all of us who have lost a loved one to gain strength and help as we walk this new path of faith. Don't do it alone, do it together!"

—Margi Galloway, Minister to Women and Spiritual Life (retired), Scottsdale Bible Church

"Comfort. . . oh, how we long for our heart to be healed when grief overcomes us. Naomi and her widow friends have been uniquely given the incredible gifts of consolation and wisdom. You and I as widows will experience both healing and restoration every time we turn a page in this anointed book."

—Glenna Salsbury, Professional Speaker/Author/Bible Study Teacher

Dedication

Ellenborg Goodman Reed
1901–1962

My godly Icelandic mother became a widow at age fifty-one when my father died suddenly. There was very little money, she could not work because of a heart condition, and she grieved the loss of her love tremendously. I suffered vicariously with her as a young teenage girl. This was the spur to start the Safe Strong Place Widows Ministry. I owe much to both Mother and my godly father, Virgil Asbury Reed.

~ Naomi

Contents

Foreword

One of my favorite women in the Bible is Tabitha (in Greek, *Dorcas*). She lived in first-century Joppa, a harbor town on the Mediterranean Sea, where the poorest of the poor were widows. These women clung to the bottom rung of society, with no one willing to protect them or provide for them. Their numbers were legion, and their ages varied. Some lost their husbands to the sea, others to illness or disease. The one thing they had in common was their widowhood.

Enter: Tabitha. She saw these women on the narrow streets of Joppa—saw their ragged clothes and their haggard faces—and her heart went out to them. Did Tabitha feed them? house them? nurse their wounds? Could be, though Scripture reveals a singular ministry for this angel of mercy: she was a seamstress. And sew she did, creating much-needed tunics and cloaks for the widows of Joppa (Acts 9:36–42).

Tabitha's story brings to mind one of my twenty-first-century role models, Naomi Rhode. She is not, to my knowledge, an expert seamstress, nor has she dressed the eight widows you are about to meet. She has, however, wrapped them in love and clothed them with compassion—listening to their stories, praying for their needs, sharing their heartaches, offering them direction, and giving each one a generous measure of hope through her online ministry.

Indeed, you'll find hope reflected in each widow's story. After the initial shock, followed by the numbness of the first days and weeks, these modern widows soon experienced the faithfulness of God in ways as different and distinctive as their individual journeys. In His Word and in their witness, it's clear the Lord holds a special place in His heart for widows, and for all who feel alone, abandoned, or adrift, even for a season.

Page by page, you'll spend time getting to know Kim, Luann, Lynda, Pam, Kathy, Marylen, Beth, Judy, and of course, Naomi. Prepare to be inspired by their stories and challenged by their courage. These women have much to teach us. And we, beloved, have much to learn from them.

~ Liz Curtis Higgs, author of thirty-seven books with nearly five million copies in print, including her bestseller, *Bad Girls of the Bible*. She has also spoken at 1,800 conferences in all fifty states and fifteen foreign countries. Liz now serves as Director of Spiritual Formation at Christ Church United Methodist in Louisville, Kentucky.

Safe, Strong Place (God)

Naomi Rhode
Jim Rhode: 4/28/36–Still here!
Married 65 years

---

*"He comforts us in all our troubles so that we can comfort
others when they are troubled. We will then be able to
give the same comfort that He has given to us."*
II Corinthians 1:4

The whirlpool was hot and bubbling, and my husband and I were relaxing together talking about *"legacy leaving"*!

We have had an amazing sixty-five years of marriage . . . yes, we were *very* young when we married. We have three children, twelve grandchildren, and expecting our eighth great-grandchildren (and counting) . . . our "quiver" is full.

We started and built a wonderful medical/dental company, SmartPractice, which is now in the capable hands of our son-in-law, a physician, and our daughter, a dentist. We have had forty-two years of professional speaking in every state and seventeen countries and are enjoying business, life, and speaking coaching. Jim was Entrepreneur of the Year in Arizona one year, we have both been President of the National Speakers Association, and I have been President of the Global Speakers Federation.

It is an abundant life filled with the richness of God's goodness and grace.

Back to "the whirlpool musing"!

Jim has always been an excellent and intuitive guide in my life choices.

So, I asked him, "Is there anything I have not done to glorify God and leave a lasting legacy?"

His reply was quick and definite: "Naomi, after your dad died when you were thirteen, you experienced ten years of loving and helping your mother in her grieving. She was ill when he died, and she lived only until you were twenty-three years old. Your mother had very little money, and life was hard. Because of that experience, you have always feared being a widow and have had a deep concern for women who have lost their spouses!

"Why not start a ministry for widows?"

I quickly shared with Jim the names of eight widows, dear friends, whom I had been praying for. These women lived in different parts of the country, and did not know each other, but all of them knew me. They had come to our seminars, heard me speak, or were speaker colleagues or friends.

They all loved the Lord, and all of them wanted to serve Him even through their grieving. They were incredible women!

After praying (always a good thing to do, I *know*), I wrote a plan and behavioral objective for a project that I had in mind.

I would have a Zoom call with widows for one hour per week. Beforehand, I would send a preamble, subject, scripture, and or commentary on the subject and questions for them to be prepared to answer on the call.

I would take the first five to seven minutes to set the agenda for the call, have prayer, and then each woman would spend time answering the questions.

I sent this proposal to the eight women, and *all* of them said *yes*.

We were off and running!

We are in our second year and fortieth week of our weekly Zoom meetings . . . with almost everyone on each of the calls!

These gals are outstanding women of God . . . with purpose, passion, and pizzaz . . . and have bonded incredibly into a fantastic "group" of supportive, caring people.

This past fall, we held a three-day retreat in a hotel in Scottsdale, Arizona.

It was a "wow" experience when they finally met in person, ending with a boat ride on an Arizona lake (yes, we do have some of those), releasing balloons with our prayer for guidance, and goals to further develop and glorify His Kingdom.

We named the group "Safe Strong Place (God)."

We wanted it to be, indeed, a "safe, strong place" of vulnerability, security, and accountability. And . . . God is the ever-present "place" where we come together. . . in His grace, His goodness, and for His glory!

My goal has been (from the beginning) that more groups like this would start. I am very supportive of grief groups that meet in churches. I also know that these small "single focused groups" can have an openness that a larger group may not be able to have, and a specificity that also may be difficult in a larger context.

When this book project was suggested, we all were delighted. This book is designed to be used as a group or individual study for those facing loss.

Now, it is up to you, dear reader, to take up the banner.

God is very clear in His desire that we include in our life legacy the concern, care, and prayer with and for widows. In James 1:27 we read:

> *"Religion that God our Father accepts as pure and faultless*
> *is this: to look after orphans and widows in their distress*
> *and to keep oneself from being polluted by the world."*

I have carefully kept all our agenda outlines so that you have a "blueprint" to use, should you desire.

> *"To God Be the Glory" is my life theme. . .*
> *May it be so, through us, this book,*
> *And now, through you!*
> *Amen and Amen*

The Loss of a Spouse

Kim Harms

"But Ruth replied, 'Don't urge me to leave you or to turn back from you. Where you go, I will go, and where you stay, I will stay. Your people will be my people, and your God my God.'"
Ruth 1:16

According to the United States Census Bureau, 75 percent of married women will become widowed, and the average age for women to become widowed is around sixty. I never paid much attention to widowhood statistics until I became one eighteen months ago.

Fifteen percent of women in the United States are currently divorced. Although their loss is similar, there are fewer resources and frequently less sympathy shown for their loss of a spouse and family as they had known it, both at the time of the divorce and when the former spouse dies.

Society today does not prepare us for a time in life when we live alone. Most of us are not ready. In our death-denying culture, we make assumptions and plan for a life lived together with our spouses. We typically do not prepare for the shock, grief, loss of identity and social standing, economic insecurity, and loneliness that frequently accompanies the loss of our life partner.

But God prepares us. The Bible contains an entire chapter focused on the plight of two widows: Ruth, who is young, and Naomi, who is not.

Naomi, having lost her husband and her two sons, is understandably bitter at first. She doesn't even want her former friends and family to call her by her name:

> *"Don't call me Naomi,' she told them. 'Call me Mara. . .*
> *for the Almighty has made me very bitter. I went away*
> *full, but the Lord has brought me back empty. Why*
> *call me Naomi, since the Lord has afflicted me, and*
> *the Almighty has brought misfortune upon me?'"*
> *Ruth 1:20–21*

But, in time, Naomi softens and begins to focus on the living, her daughter-in-law and fellow widow Ruth. Leaving our past life and expectations behind is a complex but necessary step to healing, and it is critical in our journey to accepting God's plan for our lives . . . even the painful parts.

At the end of the Book of Ruth, Naomi revels in the care of Ruth and Boaz's son, who would become the grandfather of King David and eventually an ancestor to Jesus.

Trusting and accepting God's plan for our lives can be difficult, but I have found that He is always faithful. One of the ways He has shown His faithfulness to me was to put a Naomi in my life.

My husband, Jim, and I were dentists and practiced together for many years. Naomi and her husband, also named Jim, were superstar dental educators, and we followed opportunities to hear from them whenever they appeared in the upper Midwest. My first personal encounter with Naomi and Jim was at a seminar on Mackinac Island in 1998.

At the time, I was struggling with guilt, regret, and shame associated with an accident that resulted in the paralysis of our office manager's beautiful young fifteen-year-old daughter while under my care. She had accompanied our family on a college hunting tour and, at a beach in Santa Barbara, California, the high school junior dove into a sand bar and broke her neck. The paralysis was permanent. Our office manager was devastated and angry. She blamed me, and I blamed myself. The guilt was unbearable.

Naomi and Jim held short private sessions for attendees, and I explained my dilemma and my need for forgiveness. Naomi suggested that not everyone could forgive, especially if they did not truly understand the forgiveness and grace offered by Jesus. Naomi instructed me that I may have to accept the possibility that I would never be forgiven.

Naomi's words lifted a great weight off my shoulders and allowed me to return to my office with less shame and guilt (at least I was forgiven by Jesus) and a new perspective. Thank you, Naomi.

Twenty years later, I ran into Naomi at a meeting and expressed my gratitude for her help. She was so gracious and became my new life/professional speaking coach. This time I was able to benefit from her wisdom every month.

Naomi had shared with me that one of her greatest fears was losing her amazing husband, Jim. They had been supporting each other and working together for so long; she couldn't imagine her life without him.

On August 8, 2020, I lost my husband, Jim, to heart failure. We had been married for forty-four years. The loss was unbearable, and I was terrified of facing the future alone. God has shown me in many ways since then that I am never alone. One of those ways was an invitation from my dear friend and mentor, Naomi Rhode, to join a support group for widows that she was forming. The invitation came within a week of Jim's death. Our Naomi, God's faithful servant, put the fears of her own potential widowhood aside to help her friends face theirs. Like the biblical Naomi, she is a reminder each week to put our worries aside and to trust in God's plan as he watches over us.

Naomi's **Safe Strong Place (God)** has been my lifeline. Over the last year and a half, nine of us have met faithfully every week. In October 2021, we gathered in person for a beautiful retreat. Our meetings involve frequent laughter and crying, sometimes at the same time.

Every week we are reminded that we are never alone; God worked through His obedient servant, Naomi, to teach us that.

New Part of Life's Journey

A SAFE STRONG PLACE, GOD
NAOMI'S INVITATION

Dear Ones, and that you are!

God has been speaking to *me* about *you*!

Over and over and over again!

You are in a new time of life . . . a new part of the journey.

A portion of the journey that you did not look forward to, nor perhaps even really believed would happen—and didn't plan for.

A part of the journey that leaves you in grief.

A part of the journey that leaves you wondering . . . yet knowing that God has the answers.

A part of the journey that needs wisdom . . . yet that is not always easy to access when needed most.

A part of the journey that can be lonely . . . yet there is family, there are friends . . . but they are busy.

A part of the journey that has so many questions . . . and advisors are not always readily available.

A part of the journey where the future needs to hold purpose, peace, and promise . . . who is listening?

I am listening.

I am hearing God say, "Naomi, there are so many precious women who are without their mainstay, their husbands" (second only to their faith in God).

I would like to propose:

A Safe Support Place
To grieve, to share, to laugh, to plan, to be vulnerable, to trust!
Alone . . . you are never alone!

I do not know if that will be the name.

I do not know if you would be interested in being in this group,

I do not know the group's size, but I feel it would start with about six to ten.

Plan:

1. I will facilitate.

2. You will participate/share openly.

3. We will start with one hour once per week . . . Wednesday morning, 7:00–8:00 a.m. Pacific, 10 Eastern.

4. You may or may not know any of the other women . . . how wonderful.

5. We will start with women who are widows and have faith in Christ.

6. We will start with people I have either coached or with whom I have established dear friendships.

7. We may (or may not) enlarge the group.

8. We will have discussion topics proposed by the group or by the leader as needed.

9. I will provide the Zoom link . . . so you will need to have a camera on your computer to open the Zoom link and join.

10. I also see this as an amazing time for you to minister/ encourage others with your experiences of God's providing promises and peace.

My questions for you:

1. What are your thoughts?

2. Would you like to be part of this group?

3. Would you be willing to start this coming Wed. at 7:00 a.m. West coast time . . . 10:00 East coast . . . for one hour of introduction to each other and the potential of this group.?

I look forward to hearing from you, precious women that I love, Naomi

A Time for Weeping

Kim Harms
Husband: James Roger Harms
November 6, 1949–August 8, 2020
Married 44 years

*"Two are better than one, because they have a good return for
their labor. If either of them falls down, one can help the other
up. But pity anyone who falls and has no one to help them up."*
Ecclesiastes 4:9–10

I met my husband, Jim, at a picnic softball game at the University
of Maryland. I was pitching, and he claimed that he hit three
doubles and became interested as he checked me out, running
around the bases multiple times. My account of the story has
always been that he struck out three times. He would respond
that nobody strikes out in slow-pitch softball. Jim's story is far
more believable than mine!

It was the post–Vietnam War era. During the war, Jim had been
assigned a very low draft number and signed up for a stint in
the army. He served his time at the Defense Language Institute
and Military Intelligence School. He was working in Washington,
D.C., doing background checks for security clearances and had
just started back to college to finish his degree. Jim was twen-
ty-four and I was seventeen when we met.

On one of our first dates, Jim took my little brothers and me to a
university football game and then to the dairy barns on campus,

where we checked out the cows and tried milking. Jim grew up on a farm, the twelfth of fourteen children. He was tall, blond, and wore adorable John Lennon glasses. I fell for him at first cow.

We were both zoology majors. My original plan was to become a psychiatrist to save my wonderful, kind, and loving mother. When I was six years old, Mom was institutionalized with bipolar disease and was never released. Unfortunately, she died from her disease, taking her life from me just a month before I met Jim. In my despair, I decided that I did not have the emotional stamina to handle any profession where my patients could die. When I met Jim, I was in the process of evaluating my career options.

Jim wanted to be a dentist. The year was 1974, and I had never heard of a female dentist, but women were just becoming liberated from the old school of thought, and I theorized that if I became a dentist and had a good job, maybe Jim would want to marry me. One step forward, two steps back!

At the beginning of my second semester, I went to my advisor to get some counsel on the matter. Although I realized that being female would not prevent me from going to dental school, there was one barrier that might take me out of the running. All of the dentists that I knew of had ten fingers. I only had seven.

You see, while pregnant with me, my mother traveled across the country (my dad was in the military) from Virginia to California. Along the way, she stopped in her hometown of Cincinnati, Ohio. She was suffering terribly from morning sickness, and her best friend Jo (also pregnant) gave her a new drug, used extensively in Europe but still in the testing phase in the US. That drug was Thalidomide. Jo's baby was born seriously deformed and died soon after birth. I was born with only seven fingers. Six years later we would find out that Thalidomide was responsible for severe disfigurement and the loss of limbs of over ten thousand babies in Europe. My mother was institutionalized within a week of hearing the news.

After reviewing my academic record (which was all good), I asked my advisor if he thought I could be accepted into dental school with only seven fingers. He sat back in his chair for a moment smoking his cigar (this was the '70s), and then said, "Absolutely not. There would be no way you could be a dentist with only seven fingers."

His answer made sense to me. My dental dreams were over and I immediately thought I would have to find another way to convince Jim to marry me. Darn! I got up, dejected and disappointed. As I opened the door to leave, my advisor sat back in his chair, put his feet up on the desk, took a long drag on his cigar, and added one more comment, "But maybe if you were a man, they would let you in."

My heart stopped in anger! I realized at that point my advisor had no idea if I could go to dental school, and frankly, his ego was so big he didn't care. Instead of changing careers, I changed advisors!

Changing advisors was much harder in the days before computers, but after much time spent standing in line in the advising office, I got my new assignment. It was Dr. Potter. Dr. Potter was terrifying. She was a geneticist who reminded us as we sat in the big lecture hall that at least one-third of us would not be able to cut the mustard and would drop her class by the end of the semester. She looked just like the cartoon depiction of Marge Simpson's sisters in the television program The Simpsons. She had gray, Einstein-like hair, perennially tousled. She wore a pair of slender, black-framed glasses low on her nose. She also smoked and lectured simultaneously, her cigarette dangling down but not dropping as if it were Velcro'd to her lip as she spoke. I was terrified, but I was also determined.

I knocked on Dr. Potter's door and a voice much softer than usual invited me in. I asked her if she thought I could get into dental school with only seven fingers.

She sat back in her chair and thought for a minute. "I don't know," she said, "let's find out." She immediately called the University of Maryland Dental School and set up an appointment. I met with the head of the restorative dentistry department, Dr. Buchness, and he asked me if I could hold a mirror in my right hand. I said,

"Sure I can," and demonstrated my mirror-holding skills. He said, "Only one hand goes to dental school; the other holds the mirror." I was later accepted into dental school a year early, thanks to the support and encouragement of Dr. Potter. Dr. Potter was my first mentor.

Jim and I were married less than two years later, in 1976. In fact, Jim and I started dental school together as a married couple and, except for a one-year general practice residency that I took in 1984, we practiced together for the rest of our careers. My plan worked out even better than expected!

Jim and I eventually bought a practice in Farmington, Minnesota, where we raised our family. We were blessed with three beautiful children: Hillary, born in 1982, Ashley in 1986, and Eric in 1989. Our years in Farmington were blessed with the joys and struggles of typical family life.

In the fall of 2007, my brother Mike died of a sudden heart attack; two months later, Jim was diagnosed with liver cancer. Only 5 percent of those with his diagnosis live for five years. We were devastated. Eric was a senior in high school, and the girls had moved on to college and law school. We sold half the practice and hoped for a miracle. That miracle came in the form of a liver transplant in 2008. All went well, and after a six-month recovery, Jim went back to work.

But on January 31, 2009, our world and hearts exploded when our beloved son Eric, forty-five minutes after a breakup with his girlfriend, took his own life the same way my mother had when I was seventeen.

Eric was a kind, caring, compassionate, and brilliant young man. He was a National Merit Scholar and phenomenal jazz pianist. He was attending his dream school, Columbia University in New York. Eric loved Columbia. He made the Dean's List his first semester in engineering, was elected to Student Government, participated in theater, and was accepted into the Columbia Jazz program. He was on top of the world when he came home for Christmas. Two weeks later, he was gone, and our world was completely shattered.

Those affected by the catastrophic loss of a loved one are decimated by shock and despair, wondering how they can cope with the world in general and, more specifically, the daily routines of life, like getting out of bed. We can't eat, we can't think, we can't sleep, and when we do sleep, we don't want to wake up because our worst nightmare is better than our new reality. We find that for an extended period we can no longer enjoy hobbies, read, listen to the radio, or watch television. It feels like a big fishing net is strangling our hearts and pulling us under. This is the zombie phase of grief when we are seemingly alive on the outside but dead on the inside. Jim and I spent a lot of time as zombies.

About a month after Eric died, Jim and I started back to work. It is tough to return to work when you are in the zombie phase. One evening as I left the office Jim was talking to his cousin (I will call him Carl). Carl motioned me to come over, and I could tell he and Jim were involved in a spirited discussion. Carl had lost his nineteen-year-old brother many years ago. He was left in his car after a night of drinking and froze to death. Carl knew about loss. As I approached, Carl pointed his finger at me in an accusing way and said with great intensity, "Don't you *ever* let your remaining children feel that they are not enough!" Wow, how does a grieving mother respond to that? Carl was estranged from his parents, and he blamed the emotional loss of his parents on the grief they suffered after the loss of his brother. He was not blaming me. He wanted to warn me of the dangers to the rest of my family if I became chronically overwhelmed by grief.

Entrenched in my zombieness, I realized how easy that could happen if I did not take decisive action. Jim was still recovering from his transplant and my two remaining daughters, one working and one still in law school, were struggling. They needed me, and I was determined to fight, scrape, and claw my way out of the dark pit of despair I found myself in.

It took some time, in fact, years, for me to climb out of the pit. But Jim and I did find ourselves eventually able to live in the present. We grieved differently but learned to respect our differences; we did not blame each other; we were there to support each other's needs, and we focused our attention on our living children.

Shortly after Eric's death, a survivor of the Rwandan genocide sat next to me at a prayer meeting. She told me the story about how she had lost her two children and husband during that horrible time in 1994. She also told me with great joy about her new family. She had remarried and adopted two children who had lost their parents. I looked at her with my zombie eyes and thought, "How can you possibly find joy in anything?" The next week I was given a copy of the book *Left to Tell: Discovering God Amidst the Rwandan Holocaust* by Immaculee Illibagiza and my love of Rwanda began. My dear friend Pam, who had been to Rwanda, was on the board of a wonderful organization, Books for Africa. Eric loved books, especially the classics. He would frequently rescue discarded books from local libraries. Pam suggested that we send a library of books to Rwanda through Books for Africa. She helped raise the money and in 2011 we were able to visit Rwanda and fund seven libraries, including a dental library and, through the help of Thompson Reuters, two complete law libraries. The greatest gift, however, was to me, as I was ministered to (and continue to be ministered to) by just about everyone I met there. The Rwandans realized that in order to make the country a better place for their children, they needed to do the work now when it came to justice, forgiveness, and reconciliation. Twenty-seven years later that plan has born amazing fruit. I now work with dentists and the dental school in Rwanda and continue to work with Books for Africa to bring libraries, especially memorial libraries, to villages all over the country. At this writing, there are about fifty libraries with over 300,000 books in the Eric Harms Memorial Library System.

Although we started out as a family of five, we learned to accept and focus on our family of four. By 2020 with the addition of two wonderful sons-in-law and six grandchildren (including another little Eric), we had expanded to a family of twelve. The fog was finally lifting but Eric's absence would always be felt.

After Eric's death, I was successfully treated for depression. I will take antidepressants for the rest of my life, and I am so thankful for their existence. In my case, they work. Jim, my stubborn Norwegian, would not even consider being evaluated for depression. I believe that was a costly mistake. Before his transplant, Jim's heart was strong. The year after Eric died, he underwent a nine-hour heart surgery, which included a quadruple bypass and a valve replacement. During the next ten years he suffered more heart hospitalizations, including another valve replacement, an internal bleeding incident where he lost half of his body's blood, numerous diabetic comas, a close call involving hospitalization for the flu, and an incident of septic shock where his temperature went up to 106, he had a heart attack, was put into a coma, and ventilated for several days. During those ten years, we celebrated only two birthdays in which Jim had not almost died during the previous year.

Jim bounced back so many times that I was a bit in denial when he started to decline for the last time. Jim started to fall. His blood pressure would unexpectedly decline when he stood up. In June he broke his shoulder and after several weeks of hospitalization, rehab, home, and hospitalization again, we began to see the writing on the wall. Jim decided that he wanted to come home, and thanks to the wonders of hospice, he was able to. We were even able to spend a week at the lake with all the grandchildren. It was a privilege to take care of him those last weeks. Jim's sisters, Judy, and Sue, helped out and other family members showed up for visits. On what would have been Eric's thirty-first birthday, Jim stopped breathing suddenly, with no apparent stress, as I was getting him out of the bath. I panicked and even though he was DNR (Do Not Resuscitate), I gave rescue breathing for at least five minutes. It did no good and Jim took no breaths and had no pulse. I called hospice, left a cryptic note to my dear friend Darlene, and called my daughter Hillary in tears. As we cried together on the phone for at least fifteen minutes after he stopped breathing, Jim suddenly took a big, deep breath. It was just like in the movies. I screamed, "He's alive," and dropped the phone. Seconds later, the hospice nurse arrived to console me. Again, I shouted, "He's alive," and she quickly got to work. She called rescuers to get Jim into bed. Although Jim was now breathing, he was not conscious. Eventually he regained consciousness, by this time comfortably positioned in his bed. Jim was extremely weak but fully conscious.

That day was a miraculous gift. I was able to contact family members and let them know that Jim was near the end. The rest of the day was filled with daughters, sons-in-law, sisters, brothers, nieces, and nephews visiting Jim to say goodbye. The out-of-staters showed up on Zoom. Jim had a brother who had not talked to him for years. On that day they were able to reconcile. What a precious moment that was! Jim took his final, quiet, peaceful breath early the next morning on August 8, 2020.

Even though I had been emotionally preparing for Jim's death for over ten years, I was not ready. My zombie life began again. Fortunately, I was surrounded by earthly angels, family, and friends who took care of me. Judy and Sue spent the first night with me and Ashley stayed the week. My book club friends ministered to me. We were able to have only the third post-COVID funeral at our church, which was filmed and made available to a wider audience.

Becoming a widow was not a part of my life plan, but it was God's plan and I had to accept it. After forty-four years of marriage, I now had to face life alone. Or so I thought.

One week after Jim died, I received an invitation from another angel, Naomi Rhode, to join her widow's support group, A Safe Strong Place. To me, this was a clear message from God that I was in His hands and never alone.

God Is Our Safe Strong Place

Safe Strong Place (God)
Naomi

I.

Good morning, precious friends!

This is your Safe Strong Place!

II. Journal

Keep notes of each session . . . so you can review them, and just perhaps share them with someone else who can use them!

Devotions yesterday . . . we were in Flagstaff . . . sitting on the patio overlooking the tops of all the pine trees . . . so beautiful.

I decided to name this "the Place of the Pines"! (I love naming things. . .)

Then, I found that the Hebrew word for place (hope you are writing this down) is *ha-makom*, another word for God!

So . . . all of a sudden, the name of my patio devotional spot was not just "the Place of the Pines" . . . It was "God of the Pines"!

And . . . the name I have given our group is "Safe Strong Place" . . . so unless we change the name, it can also be "Safe Strong God"!

III.

Then, I opened the Psalms at random . . . to **Ps. 116**:

> *"I love the Lord, for He heard my voice;*
> *He heard my cry for mercy.*
> *Because He turned His ear to me,*
> *I will call on Him as long as I live.*
> *The cords of death entangled me,*
> *the anguish of the grave came over me;*
> *I was overcome by distress and sorrow.*
> *Then I called on the name of the Lord:*
> *'LORD save me!'"*

IV. Prayer

Precious Father . . . we love the words of Psalm 39. We cling to your promises, Lord, that we can call on you in our distress. We can know that you weep with us at the time of deepest personal sorrow, the loss of our loving spouse. We praise your name for these wondrous words from David's heart to you, and now they are the words of our hearts to you.

We love you, Father, Amen.

You are strong women, brave, bold-called, and, yes, often sad, lonely, and wondering, but always trusting a sovereign God!

You are women of resilient strength!

V. Questions

I am anxious to hear from you! I am just a facilitator for you to teach each other.

1.

1. How is the grief journey going for you? Who do you share your grief journey with . . . your children? your friends?

2. What is your greatest need right *now*? We will pray!

Several of you have been faced with the journey of cancer. I heard Les Brown say, "The doctor said, 'You have prostate cancer, and it has metastasized to seven places.' Then I said, 'I give you the diagnosis, God, and you decide on the prognosis.'"

Powerful.

God's Cottage of Light

Luan Jackson
Husband: Thomas D. Jackson, DDS
May 11, 1945–July 18, 2020
Married 52 Years

"And he said, 'Blessed be the Lord God of my master Abraham,
who hath not left destitute my master of his mercy and his truth."
Genesis 24:27 (KJV)

I think the most important thing to know about me is that I am normal. I cry, I laugh, I get angry, and I can be cantankerous. The abnormal part about me is that I was raised in Africa, I fled the communist party at age thirteen, I speak an African dialect, I can carry water on my head, and I can pound manioc. After my family and I returned from Africa, I had a period of normal American teen life. I finished high school, I went to college, I got married, I had two children, and I started an amazing career. My human desire was to have at least four children, but God had a different plan. I spent ten years having miscarriages and stillbirths, then our seven-year-old son almost died in a go-kart accident. We worked through some financial reversals and rebuilt our business into a thriving, successful dental practice.

Before I share my career, I want to be clear that my family came first. I have been privileged to schedule my work hours around my children's school schedules. I enjoyed the freedom to take most of the summers off, and I did not start traveling until my children had graduated from high school. I also need to add that my professional career has spanned fifty years. The Bible says that the old women should teach the younger women. I tell everyone that I have reached the privilege of defining myself as an older woman and I now have the right to teach!

My career started with a bachelor's degree in nursing. I moved into management and became director of nursing of a sixty-bed facility. The State of Michigan enticed me away from that arena with an offer to become a pediatric nurse practitioner. I spent fourteen years in private practice with children and then went back to school to obtain my master's degree in psychology. I became a family therapist and established a private practice as a mental health therapist. I am nationally board-certified, and I am currently finishing a Ph.D. program. I am a professional speaker and have presented seminars on every continent except Antarctica (I need to book some time with the penguins!). I describe myself as a "people builder" and seek to encourage through one-on-one contacts, seminars, and writing. As my husband's practice grew, I used my background to manage his office. Together, we were successful, productive, and blessed.

Tom was at the peak of his dental career, our son had joined the practice, and we had plans for expansion. One day, as we were enjoying a steak dinner, I noticed that Tom was holding his knife in a strange way. He said nothing was wrong and that he was just tired. Later we found out that his hand was not good and in fact, he had ALS (Lou Gehrig's disease). He was given two years and his dental career was over. The disease took his health and his ability to take care of himself, but it could not take away his joy and positive attitude. He said one day that every night when he went to sleep, he knew that he had just had the best day he would ever have for the rest of his life, and the next morning something else wouldn't work. In spite of that knowledge, he told everyone that he had lived an incredible life. He had no regrets, and he did not have anything left on his bucket list. When friends came to visit, he talked to them about their lives and often had them laughing. Most would leave the house saying they came to cheer Tom up, but he had cheered them up. He helped plan his funeral, arranged to give everyone a copy of *The Four Spiritual Laws* from Campus Crusade for Christ, and dictated an insert for the booklets (see the appendix where the Four Spiritual Laws are written out).

"This booklet changed my life. I was a senior in college, getting ready for a night out when I stepped into the fraternity living room and heard about the spiritual laws. That night I accepted Jesus as my Savior and a sense of peace washed over me. That peace took me through dental school, marriage, fatherhood, a career, and now that peace is with me in ALS. Dear friend, please read this booklet and experience Jesus for yourself. You will not be sorry."

About a week before his actual death, his body appeared to be dying. I was watching him, praying, and preparing for the next step. Suddenly, he woke up and said, "I have been to heaven." He described a place full of light and peace. My first response was, "Why did you come back?" He just said he didn't know. Later, he shared the story with his chaplain, and I again asked why he came back. The chaplain inserted, "Because he is totally submissive to the will of God in his life," and sang the old hymn "I Surrender All."

The next Friday night, I stayed by his bed. He periodically would call my name and I would assure him I was still there. At 4:00 a.m., in a loud voice, he said, "Hallelujah, I'm almost there!" He started talking and when I asked whom he was talking to, he responded, "Jesus," as though everyone talks to Jesus. He weakened on Saturday, and we knew Tom's earthly life was coming to an end. He would sleep, then rouse and the comments he made showed his character. The first comment was about the business and how good a dentist our son was; this was Tom's commitment to his *profession*. The second time he spoke, he asked if I had been able to get his insurance money which indicated his dedication to being a good *provider*. The third comment was to ask if the doors were locked and showed his lifelong *protection* for his family. His final words were, "I love you," a fulfillment of his wedding vows. He peacefully looked up, took the hand of Jesus, and walked into heaven.

I believe my grief journey started with the deaths of my babies and the near-death of my son. I learned to trust God and rest in peace. Oh, don't get me wrong, I have cried many times, and I have spoken of my frustration as well as my anger. However, I come back to the fact that God is in control. I have also been blessed by the vision of Jesus being with me. He sat beside my bed when I gave birth to a baby without a heartbeat, He held the hand of my son in the emergency room, He cried with me when I was frustrated with the circumstances of life, He celebrated my wedding day, He smiled when we enjoyed his creation through boating, He was *always* present, and He certainly was there when Tom was ushered into heaven.

I am independent. I have traveled the world alone. I make decisions. I am proactive and a problem solver. However, I collapsed in tears the first time I tried to add a leaf to the dining room table alone. I cried when I was physically incapable of cleaning the grill. It is the jobs requiring physical strength that are most difficult for me. My solution has been to find handymen for hire.

I miss physical touch. The rolling over in bed and hugging. Holding hands while walking. The feel of a hand on the small of my back. Kissing. The intimate times. I am learning to visualize Jesus with me, holding me, comforting me; however, I crave human touch.

Another challenge is the loss of discussion. I miss having someone to dialogue with, to talk with, to communicate with. I have friends who love to talk, but no one understands me as well as Tom did. I'm working on trusting Jesus to speak into my soul.

My husband was a dentist and loved to take his staff to practice-building seminars. One day in the 1980s, he showed me a flier and said we needed to go to this program. I didn't look at it and merely agreed that if it looked interesting to him, then we should sign up. We made all the arrangements and went to the course. The hotel dining room was packed that morning and the venue was short-staffed. We were worried about getting our food and making it to the program; however, instead of worrying, we noticed a guest getting coffee pots and going around to tables filling cups, then he was helping the waitress serve food. The tension in the dining room seemed to diminish and the guests started helping each other. We eventually got to the conference room, managed to get all our staff seated together, and settled back with a sigh of relief. A lady started the program with energy and charisma not usually seen in dentistry. After a few minutes, she said, "Right now, you are probably wondering, who is this Naomi Rhode? Well, let me introduce myself. I am a dental hygienist, I have three children (Mark, Beth, and Kathy), I live in Arizona . . . but most importantly, I am a child of God." Did I hear that correctly? Did she just tell a secular audience that she was a believer? Then her husband got up, and we realized he was the man orchestrating help in the dining room at breakfast. Jim started his session with the words, "This is where dentistry is headed in the next decade unless, of course, the Lord comes back first." We were enthralled with the energy, the commitment to dentistry, the pertinent information, and the obvious commitment to God. Needless to say, we signed up for every class from that point forward. We even spent a month together in China and the South China Sea. Naomi and I shared a dressing room when we shopped, we bought fur coats the same day, and we shared speaking experiences at the National Speakers Association.

When my children were little, I wanted to be like Naomi, traveling and influencing others from the platform. God revealed to me that Naomi was living His direction for her life and that my direction was to stay home and raise my children. However, He directed me to pray for Naomi, and for many years, I knew Naomi's schedule better than her children. I knew where she was and when she was scheduled to speak. I committed to spending the entire time in prayer and felt blessed to be part of such an awesome ministry. Naomi experienced the privilege of the platform, while I experienced the privilege of intercessory prayer. What a gift!

One day after Tom died, Naomi called me and asked if I would like to be part of a grief support group. The format sounded uplifting and because the group met via Zoom, I did not have to worry about seeing the ladies the next day. While this would not be a problem for most women, I am a mental health therapist with an active practice, and the thought of being vulnerable with people I saw regularly did not sound like something I could accomplish.

The most incredible benefit for me has been the awareness that I am normal! We listen to each other, support each other, and pray for each other. What better environment for healing could possibly be constructed?

During week four we discussed places where we lived. There are so many memories associated with the places we have lived. There was married housing with paper-thin walls and the stress of trying to merge two lifestyles. There was the mobile home that was our first purchase together. It created the ability to move after Tom graduated and served us well. Then there was the fixer house that Tom bought on the golf course without telling me. I shed multiple gallons of tears over that house, but it started me on a lifetime of remodeling, DIY projects, and decorating. Then we found the perfect home on a lake, surrounded by trees, with room for us to grow as a family. Rather, God found the house for us. We were looking for a house and had found nothing suitable.

One day my mother called and said, "Your house is on the market." She went on to explain that the hostess mentioned they were listing the house the next day and my mother said, "It is the house you keep describing." We looked at the house the next day, bought it, and loved it for thirty-six years. At this point, my husband started talking about buying a retirement house up north. I did not want to move but agreed to look. God took us to a bank-owned property that was perfect in every way! I am so thankful I submitted to my husband's desire and allowed God to direct us. We had twelve magical years in the home before my husband developed ALS and died. Where I currently live is another God-directed move. Our magical house up north sold quickly, and we chose to move to a smaller, wheelchair-accessible house. I was not happy with the forced sale of our beautiful home and the move into a "compromised" house.

One night I had a dream where I was totally lost. I had spoken to a large group during the day and left town without checking directions (I tend to be impetuous). As I drove farther from town, my situation became tense, and I wanted to find something familiar. I saw a small lane leaving the main road and took it with the idea I could turn around. It was too small to allow for turning around, but I saw a cottage with light streaming out. The cottage was inviting, and I found myself wanting to go in. I stopped my vehicle and started walking to the house when a gentleman came out. I recognized him as the AV person who had helped me all day. I said, "What are you doing here?" and he replied, "I live here; this is my cottage." I immediately recognized that the man was God. He had been taking care of me all day and here He was, meeting me in my moment of need. I then realized that the cottage behind him looked like my house. The difference was that my house was dark and cold; His was bright and charming. I made a decision to create God's Cottage of Light. I want this home to be warm, inviting, and loving. I want all to see this home and know that God Himself dwells here. This house is not inhabited by my earthly husband and me; it is lived in by my heavenly husband.

A house that I would never have chosen to buy has become a blessing and a refuge for me. This is truly God's cottage of light.

Lived in Places/Loved in Places

Safe Strong Place (God)
Naomi

I.

Good morning, dear ones . . .

I hope your week was spent with family, friends . . . and yes, yes, with the Lord!

Our youngest child, Katherine, and her husband, Ken Magnuson, have moved into their newly purchased home in Phoenix from Louisville, Kentucky, this week . . . after living on Edgewater Road in Louisville for twenty years.

No big deal, you may say? Why are we talking about that today . . . ?

This is a time of huge change for Mother and Father . . . new jobs . . . new neighbors, new climate, new church . . . after twenty years of the familiar . . . the tried and true.

In essence that is what *you* experienced in a mega form when you lost your precious spouse!

Everything is new . . . new responsibilities, new location (perhaps), new empty spaces that were once filled. Maybe you got the "closet space" you always wanted (but not getting it that way). Whether it has been weeks, months, or many years, there are "boxes unpacked," or "boxes to be packed," there are forms to be filled out still . . . endless forms . . . and all the knowing that is needed continuously that you shared with your spouse before.

II.

I will get back to that as we finish today, but first we get the "best part" of our call, and that is some of the promises from God's Word . . . and your sharing:

Psalm 108 is so beautiful:

> *My heart, O God, is steadfast;*
> *I will sing and make music with all my soul.*
> *I will awaken the dawn"*
> *For great is Your love, higher than the heavens;*
> *Your faithfulness reaches to the skies.*

Psalm 112: a promise:

> *Surely the righteous will never be shaken;*
> *They will be remembered forever.*
> *They will have no fear of bad news;*
> *Their hearts are steadfast, trusting in the Lord;*
> *Their hearts are secure, they will have no fear;*
> *in the end they will look in triumph on their foes!*

III.

Our grandson, Karl, who lives and works in D.C., calls it a "love letter" to 10503 Edgewater Rd., Louisville, Kentucky. What is he really saying with these words?

> *Yesterday my family packed up the last of over two decades of life in Louisville and drove off toward a new beginning. This is my love letter to 10503 Edgewater Road, and the life lived there. Our life is rooted in geography, it is lived in places. Regular places of*

experience. Holy places of loss. Precious places of pain. Mundane places of joy. Sacred places of communion. This house, as you might observe for three minutes, was an anchor point, central geography for me. If you have spent time at this house since we moved here in 2001, I hope this blesses you as you blessed us with your presence and parallel living.

But also, this is as much an offering of thanks to and for my parents who may not have built the house, but built a home.

This is the epilogue to a "project" as their son, that I will labor through over the next twelve-plus months. I share the end now because most of our "ends" during our tenure on earth are simultaneously beginnings. In this worst of years, leaving and loss. I offer this simple visual prayer. A bittersweet ending that precedes a new beginning.

He has made
everything beautiful
in its time.
He has also set eternity
in the human heart;
yet no one can fathom
what God has done
from beginning to end.

For next week . . . I want you to think about the loss of your children . . . grandchildren . . . or siblings/friends when your spouse went home to Jesus.

There are "places" (in quotes) that you have to say goodbye to, and places that they have to say goodbye to . . . especially places of the heart.

IV. Prayer

Father, this has been a time of review of your faithfulness in the midst of enormous losses, change, and new spaces.

May we honor your faithfulness by "filling these new spaces" with beauty, peace, solemnity, music, flowers, family, friends, worship, and praise.

May we return your faithfulness . . . oh Lord, with your leading and wisdom.

Amen and amen.

VII. Questions

1. Make a list of the places you lived with your spouse, from the very beginning of your marriage.

2. Either name those places with some prominent memory, or list a few of the most poignant/powerful memories in that place.

3. How could you present this in a meaningful way as part of your marital learning legacy to family members?

4. Did you discover any surprises doing this exercise?

5. How did it make you feel?

Blessings, Naomi

Be Still, Have Quiet Rest, and Trust in the Lord

Lynda Hislop
Terence James Hislop
Birth: 12/21/1963
Death: 12/26/2018 (age 55)
Married: 27 years

"The Lord is good, a refuge in times of trouble.
He cares for those who trust in Him."

Nahum 1:7 (NIV)

I am a Minnesota girl, born in the northern city of Crookston, Minnesota but raised outside of the Twin Cities in Farmington, Minnesota. My dad, Stan Otness, was a teacher and coach. My mom, Shirley Otness, was a speech therapist. I have an older brother, Leon Otness, of three years.

We were a close family. We each had our assigned seats at the dinner table and enjoyed a family meal each night. My parents impacted me greatly. They passed on their faith to me. Faith was the foundation of our family life and our weekly schedule reflected this. There were church activities Sunday morning, Sunday evening, Wednesday evening, and anything else in between.

The next family priority was athletics. My brother and I played and competed in a variety of sports. My dad coached, sometimes, the teams we played on. My mom was our great cheerleader supporting our efforts, driving us, and attending our games. (PS: Academics were important too!)

I participated in athletics at a time when it was common to play a different sport each season. I loved the variety. Tennis in the fall, basketball in the winter, and golf in the spring and summer. While I worked hard in all three sports, golf became my primary focus and earned me an athletic scholarship to the University of Minnesota. I played on the team for four years and was captain in my final year. While competing at the Division I level was exciting and rewarding, my career was a disappointment and a struggle. This taught me that life could be hard and throw you curveballs.

It was my passion for golf that helped catch the attention of my future husband, Terry Hislop. Terry loved golf as did his family. It didn't hurt that I beat him in a basketball game of HORSE on one of our early dates.

After dating for three years, we married on November 9, 1991. We were young, ambitious, and had an exciting future planned. It was during this time that I experienced my first great loss. My father's name was on the wedding invitation and the hope was that he would live to walk me down the aisle. His battle with cancer was lost in September, about six weeks before the wedding date. My grandpa filled in as the father of the bride.

I will never forget the strength and courage my father showed throughout his battle. It provided a lasting impression of how I would handle future challenges in my life. I'll never forget the pain of seeing my strong father, the person I looked up to, cherished and worshiped, become so weak and needy, yet peaceful knowing his next home was heaven. This was a significant time for managing pain and loss.

I will never forget the strength and courage my mother showed as she journeyed through the health challenges with my dad and then entered a life of widowhood at age fifty-four. Hard to believe that I would walk in similar footsteps about thirty years later, becoming a widow myself at age fifty-three. Loss is universal.

After we married, Terry and I moved a few times due to our careers but came to call Phoenix, Arizona, home. This is where we had our twin boys, Joshua and Benjamin, built our careers, and established roots at Scottsdale Bible Church. Terry was an attorney and I was an executive for a media company.

I didn't imagine a life that would include becoming a widow at age fifty-three, with seventeen-year-old twin boys and a sweet yellow lab. But who would? Mine is a story of sudden, unexpected tragedy. The date was December 21, 2018. Terry's fifty-fifth birthday. The boys had school that day and the plan was to enjoy one of Terry's favorite meals together after school, go on a family hike and then come back home for a birthday cake. It was a beautiful day in Phoenix, Arizona, and perfect for a hike.

After an early dinner of homemade spaghetti, each of the boys read their birthday letter to their dad. This was our tradition. As parents, when it was a birthday or any holiday, what we enjoyed most from our boys was a personal note, read out loud and then kept as a keepsake. These notes were short but packed with meaning. Reminding us of good times, the special bond of parent and child, and with Terry, his great sense of humor and being such a fun dad was often emphasized.

The meal was eaten, the cards read, and it was time to go hiking. Terry was not a good "boy scout" and would often get ahead of us when hiking. This time was no different. We lost sight of Terry but knew we would see him at the end of the hike like we always did. Except this time was different. The hike ended and there was no Terry. It was dark out and Camelback Mountain was a trail that closed at sunset. There was no one else around and I immediately sensed that something was wrong. I can be slow to react, but I knew this was different. The police were immediately called, and the search and rescue began.

We had no family in Arizona but had deep ties to our church, along with a wonderful group of friends, neighbors, and business associates. Our church ties included a home fellowship group that we hosted for many years at our house. I immediately texted them and even though it was now late in the evening, they all quickly met us at the trailhead to provide much-needed support.

The search-and-rescue team did their thing in the dark with headlamps and heavy equipment on their backs. They hiked both sides of the mountain and checked the spider trails, those trails that weave off of the main trail and can cause people to get lost or, worst case, fall. They checked this difficult trail twice with no success. We were told that if he was on or near the trail he would have been found. We were told that no further attempt could be made until sunrise when there would be sunlight to see, which was about six hours away. We left the trail in a state of shock, went home for a short evening that I can't really remember, and I returned about 6:00 a.m.

That morning, the search-and-rescue team grew to include a helicopter, several cop cars, a few firetrucks, and other vehicles. It's a bit of a blur, but as some time passed the emergency vehicles increased, which I sensed was not a good sign. Then a van showed up that included a grief counselor, an even more dismal sign. Terry was eventually sighted by a helicopter. His body temperature was read remotely, and he was declared dead. I fell to the ground in disbelief.

Someone drove me home. I have no recall who it was. I had many friends with me at this time and am forever grateful for them. The family was called, church leaders were notified, a friend was called, but then, a knock on the door. Police notified us that once they reached Terry after a very technical and difficult rescue, they found a pulse. He was alive and we needed to rush to the hospital. This was after we believed he was dead for over an hour.

Off to the hospital, we went, along with many friends. I'll never forget all the people that walked alongside us providing comfort, food, encouragement, and strength when we had none. Remember, the accident was December 21; it was now the 22nd, only two days until Christmas Eve.

The boys and I were in a state of shock. I still can't recall all the details three years later and at this point never will. I do know that many surgeons and doctors tried to save Terry but there was never much hope. By the 24th, Terry's body made it clear it was time to get promoted to heaven. I was advised not to remove his oxygen on Christmas, but the day after on the 26th. This avoids the obvious clash of celebrating Jesus' birth and remembering Terry's death on the same day.

Terry passed away peacefully on the afternoon of December 26, surrounded by family and friends. He was an organ donor, and I would learn about a year later that Terry's kidney saved the life of a mother who was a staple in her community. I was sent a note by the grateful husband and the recipient that I cherish. Terry's kidney donation went even deeper for me as it was about thirty years prior that a kidney donation extended the life of my father.

On the day I became a widow the journey immediately started on how to own this new identity while staying strong for my seventeen-year-old twin boys who needed to finish their senior year of high school.

My grief journey has included tremendous acts of kindness by people I knew and didn't know. As the person on the receiving end, I've experienced the importance of stepping up to do things for others in need and not waiting to be asked. It has been a time of immense growth, a strong desire to seek God more intently, along with deep loneliness, sadness, and the lingering question of, "How did this happen to me?"

I knew I could not go this alone. My friends and family knew I could not do this alone. I immediately sought out church resources. Just a few weeks later I joined "Grief Share," a group that met weekly to help with the grieving process. After that, I requested a Stephens Minister from the counseling department at our church. These all helped me make sense of what I experienced, but it sure didn't erase the pain and loneliness.

The remaining months of my boys' senior year of high school were busy with track meets, prom, senior parties, and senior trips. All wonderful distractions. Along with my own grief, I was worried about my boys. How were they feeling and processing their dad's loss? What would be the lasting effect of this trauma?

It's important for me to keep Terry's memory alive through conversation, hanging up his traditional Christmas stocking, or having a memorial birthday lunch at his favorite restaurant. The heaviness of his loss is felt most during special celebrations or in a moment when I can tell the boys just want their dad to put his arm around them and provide the type of insight only a father can.

My concern over my boys' grief continued. Were they processing what happened and healing? Were they equipped to leave for college in the fall? Then there was a God moment. Last minute my boys joined a friend for his summer high school church camp on the beach in California. It was here that they were randomly paired with two youth leaders in their early twenties. The leaders shared they lost their dad in their teens. This led to Josh and Ben shedding some tears and talking with someone they knew understood. I sensed the healing that took place.

The boys left for college in the fall. In eight months, I had gone from a house full of activity, a central gathering place for high school boys, to living alone with our dog. I enjoyed my career and was happy to put in long hours to pass the time, but every day was still met with an evening of quietness, sadness, and loneliness. There were days when it seemed like all I could do was sit in a chair and do nothing.

I knew I needed to stay busy, and through this tragedy, my yearning for God only grew. I stayed involved in church, added another volunteer activity to my weekly schedule, and became obsessed with hiking. Hiking was an opportunity to observe God's beauty, think, push myself physically, and spend time with friends. A great day was work, hiking until sunset, showering, dinner, and sleep. I had finally figured out how to fill the void of those lonely evenings, at least on many of the nights.

A friend of mine who was consistently challenging herself physically invited me to join her and some others to train for a hiking event. We would hike seven Phoenix peaks, in one day, about a twelve-hour activity. I instantly felt purpose, community, and the excitement of working toward a goal. This led to many more training hikes and feats with what became a group of ladies that unquestionably helped me survive my losses and the isolation of COVID.

My biggest widowhood challenge is doing life alone after having a husband and life partner of over thirty years, along with a tremendous amount of change in less than two years. Over a twenty-month period, I lost my husband, my twin boys left for college, the dog died, and my twenty-two-year executive career with a company full of people I adored came to an abrupt and unforeseen end. I still remember the call from my company vividly to tell me the news. I had a good friend to shed some tears with, then felt the tremendous pressure to be strong for my boys and for them not to get worried or feel a lack of security now that mom was single and unemployed.

I honestly don't know how I survived, but by the grace of God and the people He placed into my life. Thank you, God, for your unwavering love and promise that all things work together for good.

I'm not like the others in the Safe Strong Place (SSP) group. I had never met Naomi. The others in the group had known Naomi for years. They attended her business seminars, she coached some of them and some were close friends. While I was an outsider to this group of accomplished women, I immediately felt welcomed, included, and safe.

Naomi and I attend the same church. It's a megachurch and we never met until SSP. She invited me to join her and Jim at their Sunday School class. I said yes, met them in person, and have continued to attend class ever since. Sitting next to Naomi each week, seeing her infectious smile, having her hold my hand, give me a hug, or say some encouraging words is a deep blessing. I treasure both her and Jim as friends, counselors, and mentors.

A dear friend of mine called and said, "You need to connect with Naomi Rhode. She's starting up a group for widows." I was thrilled about this introduction. I needed people in my life to get through this fragile time. Others that understood, were wise, strong, encouraging, and safe. Naomi and I spoke by phone, and I instantly knew this was a leader I wanted to follow. Dynamic, welcoming, insightful, wise, and most importantly, a woman of strong faith.

I thought, *what a blessing to be introduced to this new group.* A few days passed after my initial call with Naomi when I received the business call letting me know I no longer had my job of twenty-two years. I was crushed. My career was a big part of my life, identity, and the friendships I had. Not to mention the income I needed to live. The only constant in my life was a God that always provides. I put my trust in Him, along with reaching out to anyone I knew that could provide a lead for a new job. I emailed Naomi to let her know I lost my job and that I wouldn't have the right mindset to join the first SSP meeting that week. She encouraged me to join the call, show up, even if it was just to listen. I joined the call, was blessed, and instantly bonded with this group of women.

I understand that the healing process is different for everyone. What I do know is that you need people and your faith in God to heal. Our weekly call is sacred, not to be missed. Our time together is a lifeline. There have been times when I didn't know how to move forward, felt very alone, or was experiencing intense emotional pain and these women get it. We relate in a way that only fellow widows can, all grounded in God's truth.

The lesson on the universality of loss spoke deeply to me. I know we all experience loss, but I was really feeling the depth of heavy loss. I was feeling loss from every angle. My executive career of twenty-two years is gone. My financial security declined. My twin boys left for college and that natural separation was taking place. My dog of twelve years passed. Then there was the added fear of what loss was next.

It was during our SSP meeting that I was reminded and encouraged by these key takeaways:

- God wants to fill the void of loss

- God put me in this place and I'm where God wants me to be

- The places we are in only matter if God is there

- Peace equals the inward calm God produces

- Be still, have quiet rest, and trust in the Lord

> *"That day when evening came, he said to his disciples, 'Let us go over to the other side.' Leaving the crowd behind, they took him along, just as he was, in the boat. There were also other boats with him. A furious squall came up, and the waves broke over the boat so that it was nearly swamped. Jesus was in the stern, sleeping on a cushion. The disciples woke him and said to him, 'Teacher, don't you care if we drown?' He got up, rebuked the wind, and said to the waves, 'Quiet! Be still!' Then the wind died down and it was completely calm. He said to his disciples, 'Why are you so afraid? Do you still have no faith?' They were terrified and asked each other, 'Who is this? Even the wind and the waves obey him!'"*
> *Mark 4:35–41 (NIV)*

The Universality of Loss

Safe Strong Place (God)
Naomi

I.

Good morning, dear ones,

You are so faithful . . . and I am so blessed by your care for each other, and desire for the comfort and answers that true sharing can accomplish.

The theme today is: The Universality of Loss. . . No one really knows what it is all about until you know what it is all about!

When I think of the losses in my life . . . and even dare to name them . . . they are:

1. precious people

2. security of locations . . . homes

3. the realization of the stages of life . . . from birth to *now* . . . and the losses involved

4. losses in health

5. losses of relationships

One day I was asked if there was one word that describes my life, what would it be, and I said *loss*! That may surprise you because I am a *very* happy, abundantly fulfilled, encouraged, and encouraging person . . . but that seemed the reality of the summation of my life at that instance.

That person challenged me to list the gains . . . the doors opened . . . the comfort given . . . the recovery accomplished from each of the losses . . . and it was a huge change in perspective. You may want to try that!

II.

Scripture for today is Psalm 34:1:

> *"Therefore I will bless the Lord at all times . . . His praise will continually be in my mouth!"*

III.

Pam sent me these thoughts this week, and they are great:

> *"I was thinking about questions I would like to ask. Approaching are the firsts of Tom not being here (my family's birthday season, Thanksgiving, and Christmas). Everyone in my family has different feelings about what they do and don't want to do but all are dreading doing these things without him."*

IV. Prayer

Oh precious Father, we stand before you with a deep awareness of the layers of loss that have occurred in our lives. We know that you don't want us to get stuck "in the losses" . . . but to learn from them and to lean into your loving arms for perspective and comfort. We are in awe of this trust and your grace, both gifts from you to our hearts.

We love you, Lord, Amen.

V. Questions

1. What things have others done? How did they navigate the different grief responses in the kids? Any ideas about how to approach and walk through this?

2. What other questions do you have that you would like us to address?

Love and prayers for comfort and joy!

Naomi

Pam Bennett

Thomas Gordon Bennett III
September 20, 1948–July 11, 2020
Married almost 41 years

"Whoever dwells in the shelter of the Most High will rest in the shadow of the Almighty. I will say of the Lord, He is my refuge and my fortress, my God in whom I trust. Surely, he will save you from the fowler's snare and from the deadly pestilence. He will cover you with his feathers, and under His wings, you will find refuge; His faithfulness will be your shield and rampart."
Psalm 91:1–4

Tom and I both grew up in Maryland and attended a small college in western Maryland. It was the '70s and Tom was a bit of an adventure-seeking guy, so after he fulfilled his ROTC commitment, at the tail end of the Vietnam War, rather than settle into a job, he decided to travel. He went south to Mexico to experience life there, went west to Utah to take graduate classes and ski, and finally north to Alaska, where he worked fishing for halibut in the sometimes-dangerous waters off the coast. After a near-death experience during a storm at sea, God opened his eyes to the gospel and he surrendered his life to the Lord. He returned to rural Calvert County ready to settle down and start his grown-up life.

Though we had similar friends at college, we didn't date until several years after my graduation and his return to Maryland, reconnecting at a party of college friends. We started dating and fell in love. Both of us were ready for a change in career. I had been teaching special ed students in the local high school and wanted to go to nursing school; he dreamed of becoming a physical therapist. We both went back to school to make those dreams a reality. After graduation from our respective schools, we planned our wedding, eventually settling in my hometown near Annapolis. We had four children and led busy, full lives, with Tom practicing physical therapy, and me homeschooling our children. Life was good. We were very involved in our local church, leading small groups, mission trips to Guatemala, and Tom occasionally preaching. Additionally, Tom had a heart for prison ministry and for over twenty years he led weekly Bible studies in several prisons. Most of our time was spent investing in our children and in our community. We immersed ourselves in all our children loved: basketball, musical theater, music lessons, recitals, and speech and debate. In 2017, all our children were married and having children themselves—six total at the time. Tom and I were in the process of helping our daughter and son-in-law plant a church just outside of Washington, DC. Tom was running three miles a day and working fifty hours a week. Our family was all together for a family vacation in the Outer Banks that summer and celebrated birthdays in the fall. By Christmas, Tom wasn't feeling well.

On January 8, 2018, a day indelibly etched in my heart, Tom was seeing patients and doing physical therapy as he had for nearly forty years, on an abbreviated schedule because he still had a lingering GI illness the doctors couldn't seem to diagnose. He had gone to the ER the week before and had a CAT scan on the advice of our son (a radiologist in North Carolina). Results of the CAT scan were normal, the doctors said, and he was sent home. When our son received a copy of the scan in the mail, he called Tom to tell him news that would shatter our world forever. "I am 98 percent sure you have pancreatic cancer." In numbed shock and frozen fear, our entire family mobilized into battle readiness as Tom and I tried to take in the news. Each one worked feverishly in their area of gifting.

Twenty days later Tom had seen the co-director of a large pancreatic cancer center (where it typically takes six weeks to get an initial appointment) and completed all the scans and procedures he needed. Pancreatic cancer is difficult to treat. The prognosis is three months with standard care treatment so our sons researched extensively, consulted with doctors in Texas and Arizona, contacted the premier center for PC research, and secured an appointment to be considered for the clinical trial our sons thought would be his best shot. We met with our attorney, Tom notified his work, and my son and his wife moved into our home to take care of it while we were gone. We had every house and business detail taken care of: a solid prayer team was formed and praying; friends and family were notified and a system was set up to keep them informed about what was happening; clothes, records, and Tom's supplies were packed for us; tickets were purchased, and we boarded a plane for Scottsdale, Arizona in twenty days, leaving our family and friends behind.

We had no idea where we would stay or how we would finance this trip when he wasn't working. Through friends at church, God provided two lovely homes with Christian couples, both close to the cancer center where Tom received treatment. We arrived at the Rhodes' home (where we would live for five of the eight months we were in Arizona) and several days later met Jim and

Naomi for the first time. Naomi hugged me tight, smiled warmly, and said, "Sweetheart, welcome home! We want this to be an oasis of healing for you." And that is exactly what it was.

Tom and I went for his first appointment at Honor Health two days later. To be admitted to the clinical trial the doctors needed definitive proof Tom's cancer was stage 4—the worst possible end-stage cancer. That's a strange thing to pray for—"Lord, please let them find cancer in Tom's liver so he is stage 4." Though the liver scan showed two suspicious spots, biopsy proof was needed or he could not get into the clinical trial that would potentially save his life. Our son, a radiologist who did these procedures all the time, said the spots were very small and in hard-to-reach locations. He was not at all confident the radiologist would be able to get the proof we needed. We arrived at the small, underwhelming hospital, two thousand miles from our home in Maryland. The radiologist walked in casually in an LL Bean hoodie with a demeanor to match. First, they couldn't locate the scan to guide the biopsy needle to the correct spot. When they finally did find the scan he casually and dismissively said it was in a hard spot to reach and he didn't think he could do it. At that point, I was ushered to the lobby to wait and called my daughter to mobilize the prayer team. Tom told me afterward what had happened. Tom called our son to talk to the doctor; then asked if he could pray before they started. Tom said that after that prayer, the atmosphere in the room completely changed. The tech who had been irritable and impatient softened. The radiologist was now laser-focused and determined to nail the correct spot. It was tricky because it was near the lung. Tom had to hold his breath while the radiologist fed the needle up and tried to get a snip of the targeted area. After four tries, he took Tom back for a repeat CAT scan (something they *never* do) to see if the needle marks were actually in the tiny spots that were suspicious. When he determined they were, he fast-tracked the samples (something he said earlier he absolutely couldn't do) so Tom's case could be discussed in the tumor board two days later. The biopsy came back as cancer in two out of four spots and he was admitted into the "Grand Slam," baseball lingo for the five drugs Tom would be given to kill this cancer.

In the midst of this hardest challenge of our lives, Tom and I began to see God's care for us in ways we hadn't seen before Tom's illness. In the place of desperate need, we saw the Lord provide in the smallest and biggest ways, often in the eleventh hour, moment by moment. At times it was a tangible provision; at other times we only saw in retrospect His tender care. As Psalm 91 promises, the Lord sheltered us under His wing. He carried us. He took care of our needs. He was our very real refuge and comfort. Tom knew it and never asked the Lord, "Why me?" When we were the weakest, He was teaching us to trust as we never had before the tender care of our loving Father.

In early September 2018, we returned home to Maryland. Tom's tumor markers were back to normal and he was told, "Go home and live your life." But with the aggressive nature of pancreatic cancer, the fear of return always lurks in the shadows. We reunited with family and friends and Tom enjoyed ten months of living life and enjoying quality time with our children and now eight young grandchildren under seven. (Two were born while we were in Arizona!)

Two days after we returned home, we were jolted again. My daughter had a lingering concern that I might have cancer too and insisted I get scans. Most doctors would not authorize scans for worry, but my doctor did. After putting it off for three months, I finally had the scan right before we came home to Maryland because I knew she would be upset if I didn't. It seemed like overkill to me. After all, I had just had a diagnostic mammogram three weeks earlier and it was normal. The results of the CAT scan showed a suspicious lymph node. It was biopsied just before we came home to Maryland and two days after we returned my doctor called, stunned that the suspicious lymph node was breast cancer. What I didn't know was that 20 percent of breast cancers do not show up on mammograms and mine was that type. Had I not gotten the scan, the cancer would have gone undetected for another year until the next mammogram. Likely the cancer would have been stage 3 or 4 instead of stage 2. It was a miracle that it was discovered early with a high likelihood treatment would be successful. Tom had temporarily finished his chemo and we were home so I could get treatment locally and family and friends were there to help.

I had surgery and chemotherapy and was scheduled for radiation. It is hard to make sense of trial upon trial, yet during that time, I was given a glimpse of how trials teach, refine, and deepen our relationship with Him in an almost indescribable way. Elisabeth Elliott said, "The deepest things I have learned in my own life have come from the deepest suffering. And out of the deepest waters and the hottest fires have come the deepest things I know about God" (*Suffering Is Not for Nothing*, 9). Cancer was the fire that deepened my understanding of God in a way I never understood before and brought new meaning to His promise to be an ever-present help in trouble, who is with us and will never leave, who loves us with everlasting love and will work all things for good in our lives. The lessons learned through suffering changed my life for the better.

By July 2019, Tom's cancer marker was sneaking up and the scans showed early changes in the tumor, both signs of recurrence. So, in July and August, we both had radiation followed by a reprieve from the treatment for several months. In late January 2020, his health began to deteriorate, first with gallbladder problems and surgery from which he never fully recovered. Then Covid emerged and all of Tom's hospitalizations at a large teaching hospital were now solo with no visitors. Someone had always been with him, advocating, supporting, and present to help. Now he was sick and alone; the toll was heavy. He entered hospice at our home at the end of June. We prayed intensely that God would heal Tom, that the clinical trial would be successful and he would have many more years as some did. Ultimately God answered our prayers to heal him but not in the way I would have if I had written the story. Yet I know God is the author of the best story so through tears and immense grief, I trusted His plan. On July 11, 2020, with me by his side, Tom went to be with the Savior he loved and served. How grateful our family was for two and a half years instead of three months.

My grief journey began much earlier than July 11. The intense chemotherapy Tom received to kill the cancer also had physical, emotional, and mental collateral damage. It took part of "us," the way we could talk, share and understand each other and dream about the future. He felt it too but couldn't do anything about it. It's almost as if with the toxic assault on the body from chemotherapy, all bodily resources are directed to physically staying alive. This was the most difficult and painful part of the cancer journey—losing bit by bit the depth of who we were together. It was dark and lonely.

My only comfort in those days when I couldn't even pray and the suffering seemed too great was scripture. I clung to the verses of Psalm 91: "Because he holds fast to me in love, I will deliver him. I will protect him because he knows my name. I will be with him in trouble. I will rescue him and honor him . . . and show him my salvation."

In those first days after Tom died, the raw personal pain and grief were cushioned somewhat by the rally of people around me bringing food, helping with arrangements, and supporting our family, but as time passed and reality began to seep in and normal life resumed for everyone else, the place in my heart that was torn away, the dark hollowness of each minute seemed almost overwhelming. When night came, the aloneness screamed the loudest; the empty place next to me in bed brought a chill to my soul. I want to go to sleep and dream about our life together, a time before he was sick, a happy time filled with a naïve sense that we would last forever, but sleep didn't come. Memories flooded my mind, not wanting any detail of him ever to be forgotten. Frantic thoughts that I cannot do this darted through my head. Then, in that still small voice, through scripture texted to me or in the Psalms playing through the night on my phone, a reminder of

God's truth whispered to my heart. I felt the power of God's word as it interrupted the grief and sorrow and brought a deep-seated hope that His faithfulness would prevail and reminded me that as a child of God, I really am not alone because He is with me. Eventually, sleep provided a reprieve for a few hours. And so went the next days and weeks and months.

The daylight hours were just as turbulent. Everything was "us." Everywhere I turned, he wasn't there. He had my back and was by my side; he was my steady, faithful rock, my prayer warrior. He loved me, really loved me unconditionally. He was in me and part of everything in my life. I sat frozen, unable to do the things before me, insurance papers, financial and legal work, his clothes, what to do about my house, etc. I couldn't focus and think through the work in front of me. My thoughts drifted back to him, wanting more time, even one more evening. There is never enough time. Was I going crazy? Everything was different now and I wasn't sure who I was without Tom. Even surrounded by family, I felt a profound aloneness. Raw reflections of what I felt inside were softened by the words of hymns we had listened to a thousand times that reminded me God's promises are as true now as before Tom got sick. "Great is thy faithfulness, O God my father. There is no shadow of turning with thee. All I have needed thy hand has provided. Great is thy faithfulness, Lord unto me" (From "Great is Thy Faithfulness" by Thomas Obadiah Chisholm). I knew He would carry me through and in the end, all will be made new in eternity.

Naomi and Jim had welcomed us into their home two years earlier and had become close friends and mentors. We had many hours of dinners, conversation, laughter, tears, and prayer when we lived with them. When Tom needed to return to Scottsdale for doctor appointments, their home was open for him to stay. Naomi listened with her heart to my emails and calls when I was back in Maryland, encouraging me and praying for me in the sad times when I felt Tom slipping away, and times during my treatment for cancer when I felt overwhelmed in a black hole of sadness. She has a way of looking at everything in life from a glass-half-full perspective, seeing Christ and His wonderful plan for our lives in the most difficult circumstances. Her optimism is contagious.

On August 15, 2020, Naomi's email arrived asking if I would like to join a widow's support group on Zoom. She was not a widow, and in fact, her biggest fear was becoming one. Most people would run from such an opportunity, but in Naomi fashion, her empathy for those who lost husbands outweighed her fear and she gathered friends who were widows and jumped into the ring. Though I am not a group person I could hear Tom's voice in my head telling me to join the Zoom group. With some reluctance, I replied yes to her invitation. It was one of the best decisions I have made.

The group has been a lifeline for me in the turbulent waters of losing my husband. We met on Zoom each week from August 19, 2020, and are still meeting today. The group is composed of women who lost their husbands just weeks ago (like me) and others who have been widows for as long as fifteen years, bringing a rich diversity in experience and perspective. Guided by questions and a reflection by Naomi, it is a place to share openly, ask questions and think through loss using the lens of scripture, pray, discuss any problems/obstacles we have, and listen and glean wisdom from other women in different stages of grief. The commonality of feelings and struggles, the insight from others, and the prayer and support reinforce that I am not alone and validate the rollercoaster ride grieving a husband's loss can be. Though the stories of each widow revealed how God cares for believers in very different ways, we all universally can proclaim His goodness. My biggest struggle is an ongoing one of learning to live in this new reality of life as a widow, following God's leading alone. But I know with each step in the process, I have their hands, their encouragement, their ideas, and their prayers—all evidence of God's overwhelming kindness to me.

Tom, an avid runner, called his fight against cancer a marathon. In fact, the Christian life is a marathon, a journey laced with joys and hardships as we run with perseverance the race marked out for us. It is a paradox that as we go through the inevitable suffering in this life, we witness God's kindness and goodness in ways not seen before. It has been twenty months without Tom. That probably sounds like a long time, but the truth is, it still feels very fresh. The acute panic of emotion in the first weeks and months has abated but there are still nights when those gnawing gut-punch feelings of loss come and days when a trigger brings deep sadness and uncontrollable tears. Deep love and suffering are intimately connected it seems. But in this darkest time, with the most pain and most profound sorrow, most intense despair and loss, the power of God's word has spoken the loudest, and my faith and trust in God have grown the most. From Genesis through Revelation, the Bible tells His story, the story of God's love for His people and His plan to redeem this broken world through His son Jesus with a new heaven and a new earth. We are all part of His grand plan. I will never know until eternity why God designed our lives this way, but I am sure more than ever of His love, protection, and care. He walked with us through the fire and kept us under His wing. He answered every prayer, delivered us, and showed Tom His salvation. One day I will see clearly, as Tom does now, how God weaved all the threads of our lives for our good and His glory.

Suffering, Acceptance, and Peace

SAFE STRONG PLACE (GOD)
NAOMI

I.

Elisabeth Elliott lost two husbands. The first was murdered on the mission field when her baby was six months old. The second died of cancer three and a half years after they married. Yet she gratefully accepted everything in her life as from God's hand for her good. "In acceptance lieth peace." Much of what she recommends to us lies in Psalm 91:

"Whoever dwells in the shelter of the Most High will rest in the shadow of the Almighty. I will say of the Lord, 'He is my refuge and my fortress, my God, in whom I trust.' Surely he will save you from the fowler's snare and from the deadly pestilence. He will cover you with his feathers, and under his wings you will find refuge; his faithfulness will be your shield and rampart. You will not fear the terror of night, nor the arrow that flies by day, nor the pestilence that stalks in the darkness, nor the plague that destroys at midday. A thousand may fall at your side, ten thousand at your right hand, but it will not come near you. You will only observe with your eyes and see the punishment of the wicked. If you say, 'The Lord is my refuge,' and you make the Most High your dwelling, no harm will overtake you, no disaster will come near your tent. For he will command his angels concerning you to guard you in all your ways; they will lift you up in their hands, so that you will not strike your

foot against a stone. You will tread on the lion and the cobra; you will trample the great lion and the serpent. 'Because he[b] loves me,' says the Lord, 'I will rescue him; I will protect him, for he acknowledges my name. He will call on me, and I will answer him; I will be with him in trouble, I will deliver him and honor him. With long life I will satisfy him and show him my salvation.'"

"This is why as believers, though we suffer and struggle with heartaches of all kinds, we can with confidence accept whatever God allows in our lives because we know that whatever He allows is the best and what we would have wanted if we knew all the facts. One day we will know and will worship Him face to face."
Elizabeth Elliot, Suffering Is Never for Nothing

"The deepest things I have learned in my own life have come from the deepest suffering. And out of the deepest waters and the hottest fires have come the deepest things I know about God."
Elizabeth Elliot, Suffering Is Never for Nothing

"'In Acceptance Lieth Peace.' That phrase has become a dictum for me. Acceptance of my circumstances, the first step in obtaining joy and peace, begins with faith. I would have no reason simply to accept the awful things that happen if I had no idea that Somebody was governing this world and that my individual life was completely under the control of One who possesses perfect wisdom, perfect justice, and perfect love."
Amy Carmichael, In Acceptance Lieth Peace

My prayer for you, precious sisters, is that it may be so . . . *peace* . . . peace . . . peace. When I had my major stroke and was paralyzed twelve years ago, I had indescribable peace; it was amazing; *only* the Holy Spirit gives that kind of peace.

"Now the Lord of peace Himself gives you peace."
II Thessalonians 3:16

II. Prayer

Dear Father, please bring to us the peace of the Holy Spirit that passes all understanding, and allow us to trust in you and your plan for us, no matter what the circumstances. Allow us to embrace the hope of your creative purpose and understand that you are still working through us even in the wake of our pain.

Amen.

III. Sharing

1. What is your definition of peace?

2. What scripture or verses give you peace?

3. What is the connection between faith, fear, and peace?

4. When are you most lacking in peace?

5. Who is on your support system team?

6. Why is this so important? So important that we find peace in Him.

When we are not at peace, we are anxious and fearful. And, our anxiety, fear, mind, emotions, and the way our brokenness affects our life do not disqualify us from knowing, loving, and serving the Lord and from being used by Him. You and your heart and your life are a needed asset to the kingdom of God!

"God has ordained that we should gather again and
again to remember again and again who we are and
what we have been given. His church (Safe Strong Place

God) is a tool of grace, a vehicle for remembering, so that
we may celebrate and grow in His grace and peace."
Paul Tripp and Naomi

"I will be with you, and I will protect you wherever you go."
Genesis 28:15

V. Questions

Read daily, and study "The Welcoming Prayer":

Welcome, Welcome, Welcome.
I welcome everything that comes to me today
Because I know it is for my healing.
I welcome all thoughts, feelings, emotions, persons,
Situations, and conditions.
I let go of my desire for power and control.
I let go of my desire for affection, esteem,
Approval, and pleasure.
I let go of my desire for survival and security.
I let go of my desire to change any situation,
Condition, person, or myself.
I am open to the love and presence of God and
God's action within. Amen

Welcoming Prayer by Father Thomas Keating (with permission of
Contemplative Outreach)

1. What is it saying to God?

2. How does it make you feel to pray this prayer?

3. What part or parts of the prayer are different than what you would usually pray for or about?

4. What is hardest to release to Him, and why?

Kathy Dempsey

Ron Black
April 15, 1946–May 7, 2013
Married: 3 days

"Come to me, all you who are weary and
burdened, and I will give you rest."
Matthew 11:28

I was born and raised in Washington, DC, until fourteen years old when my dad quit his job at GEICO and decided to go back to school and study for the ministry, and we moved to Chattanooga, Tennessee. He had been part of the gospel singing group called the Kingsmen. After high school, I attended nursing school, then graduate school in psychology at the University of Tennessee. My graduate thesis was on death and dying, grief and loss. I worked as an ER/trauma nurse, then in hospital administration of psychiatric, educational, and Alzheimer's services.

In 2000, I started my own business full-time and became a motivational speaker and author, helping people *shed* whatever is holding them back in life, physically, mentally, and spiritually.

In 2008, I was living in the Philadelphia area and speaking all over the world. I had just come back from India and became very sick. I was speaking at a conference in Scottsdale, Arizona, and almost fainted on the stage. Naomi Rhode said, "You need to see my Dr. Lakin." After examining me and running some tests, he said, "You're grounded! For the next three weeks, cancel all your speaking engagements and flights." I was in shock! And with some resistance, I finally acquiesced.

A few days later, I met Ron Black online, and at the semi-command of my friend Kirstin whom I was staying with, Ron and I had our first date at a coffee shop called C4. I'd never laughed so much for three hours, which was healing to my body and soul.

Providentially, I ended up never leaving Arizona and moved here permanently.

Ron and I had a great relationship. We worked together, played together, and rode bikes together. He loved music, and every cell of his body lit up when he was playing or teaching kids how to play guitar. With his IT and SEO skills, my business was booming. We planned a trip to Hawaii to celebrate and fulfill Ron's dream vacation. After booking the flight and hotel, we went on a fifteen-mile bike ride. On the way back, Ron's doctor called. It was Saturday, 8:00 a.m. Never a good sign.

The doctor said, "Your lab results have come back from your routine physical. You have a panic potassium level. You're in renal failure. Get to the closest ER immediately."

Ron responded, "There must be some mistake. I'm feeling fine. I just rode my bike fifteen miles."

The doctor responded, "I've never in my thirty years of medicine seen anyone walking around alive with this kind of level. Get to the ER now."

Being a former ER nurse, I knew what a panic potassium level meant. When it gets this high, your heart goes into arrhythmias, and it stops. I drove Ron to the closest ER, a few blocks away. They took him back immediately and started an IV, EKG, and tests. In minutes, four doctors came in and said the same thing: *You should be dead! You should be dead! You should be dead! You should be dead!* And then he coded, but they got him back.

The next few weeks hit hard with surgery, the diagnosis of stage 4 renal cancer, starting dialysis, and canceling our Hawaii trip. But that didn't stop us from having a virtual Hawaii trip during Ron's hospital stay. This launched the most amazing, painful year of my life. Ron was in and out of the hospital, on dialysis three times a week for four hours, but remarkably, on the brink of death, he'd bounce back, crack a joke, and be back on his bike riding fifteen miles.

On my "Valentine's Day from Hell" date, the doctor told Ron and me, "The cancer has progressed. It has spread from the kidneys to the adrenals and pancreas, and thyroid, and bone, and lung." I interrupted the doctor and blurted out with a fierce scream, "Dr. Lui, do you have any good news? Please, I beg you, can you give me one ounce of good news?"

He glanced down at the pathology report. He looked back up at me and calmingly responded, "It's not in the brain. That's good news."

A few weeks later it was May, eleven months from the initial diagnosis. My busiest time of the year for speaking/travel. I just got off a fifteen-mile bike ride with Ron. The next day I was leaving for an intense two-week speaking schedule across the country and landed in Miami for a black-tie affair for 1,200 people.

The following day, I got a call from the dialysis clinic saying Ron never showed up. My heart sank into my stomach. I tried to call him but got no response. I tried to text him, no response. Then 911.

The police arrived. They were able to get in the house and found Ron on the bathroom floor . . . still alive two days later.

The ambulance took him to Mayo Clinic, where hours later, the neuro-oncologist called and said Ron's cancer had spread to the brain, causing severe hemorrhaging, a stroke, and paralysis on his left side.

As I was on the other end of the country, Naomi and Jim Rhode immediately headed over to Mayo Clinic to be with Ron.

I hung up the phone and started sobbing. I felt so alone. I had No one to be with me. No one to comfort me. How was I supposed to speak to 1,200 people in an hour? How was I supposed to inspire them when I could not even inspire myself to stop crying? Thousands of miles away, I opened the drawer, and there was a Gideon Bible. It seemed like a sign. Knowing Ron was in the best hands possible, I asked God for strength, went on and spoke, and then immediately flew back to Phoenix.

I walked into Ron's room in Mayo ICU with our minister. There were tubes, machines, and monitors everywhere. After giving Ron a hug, he turned to our minister and said, "I have an important question. Does Jesus have a band? I'd like to be in the guitar section. (We laughed.) I don't want to be in the tuba section. (We laughed even harder.) I better start rehearsing. It looks like I'll be starting sooner than I thought."

A few minutes later, the neurooncologist walked in and showed me the results of Ron's CAT scan of the brain. I took a deep sigh . . . it was the final gunshot wound.

So, painstakingly, I did the hardest thing I've ever done. I stood at the nurse's station and signed the papers to turn off dialysis and let Ron die. Tears flowed.

He was transferred to hospice.

Upon arrival, I asked Ron if he needed or wanted anything. He turned to me and said, "I want an interactive funeral." Perplexed, I responded, "What?" "Yes, I want to be alive at my funeral. I know it's weird, but that is why I am with you!" I chuckled and agreed.

So, we planned one for the next day, Mother's Day. Naomi was our MC for the service. Friends brought their guitars, banjos, and synthesizers. Some attended via Skype, some on a conference call, and some sent in messages on email to be read to Ron.

Ron's interactive funeral Sunday night was surreal. I have never experienced anything like it in my life. Ron had us laughing one moment and crying the next. In a wheelchair in front of the "standing room only" community center, he spoke with tears and humor. He said, "Kathy and I will be traveling together soon. I'll just be on the 'outside' of the plane."

I have been with thousands of people who have died in my life, and I have never seen anyone die this well. After the funeral, and Ron was back in his room, I turned to him and said, "Ron, you are amazing, and you are dying so well. Please tell me, how do you do this?" He said, "You die well by living well today!"

Profound!

I kissed him goodnight and headed home three blocks down the street.

I woke up early the following day, got out of bed, looked in the beveled-shaped mirror on my dresser, and said to myself, "You are getting married today!"

What?

"Yes," I confidently said back to myself. "You are getting married today." "You are crazy! I am not getting married today." "Yes, you are. Open your jewelry box, get your parents' rings, get on your bike, and go now!"

I grabbed the rings and hopped on my bike in a surreal state.

As I was pedaling faster and faster, my mouth became drier, my stomach queasier, and I started panicking. Ron and I had never talked about the "M" word. But what if he says no? A dying man? That'll be ten more years of therapy!

I arrived at the hospice, knocked on Ron's door, and walked in.

Ron slowly opened his eyes, and I sat down beside him in the bed. I kissed him on the cheek and said, "Good morning, sweetheart. I have a question for you."

I looked him in the eye. Our faces were about eight inches away from each other, and I said, "Will you marry me?"

There was a silent pause. What seemed to be three hours was, in reality, only about three seconds; he whispered back in a confident voice, "*Yes!*"

"Yes? . . . Awesome! He said yes!" I was reveling in his response when there was a knock on the door. The gentleman stuck his head in and introduced himself. He said, "Hello, my name is Barry. I am the hospice chaplain. Can I help you?"

I jokingly said, "Well . . . .do you do weddings?" and I chuckled. He said, "Yes, I do!" "Really. Can you marry us?" He said, "Yes, I have my wedding book in the back of my car. I'll be right back and get it."

I looked down at Ron and said to myself, "What are you doing? This man is eaten up with cancer, every organ of his body. He's had a stroke. He's paralyzed. He's wearing a diaper. He has a catheter. He will be dead within a few days. What are you doing, Kathy Dempsey?"

Suddenly, I looked into his eyes and realized that this man was the most beautiful man in the entire world. Then, I looked down at myself. I was dressed in my bright green long-sleeved SHED NOW t-shirt, black biking pants, and green tennis shoes. No makeup, hair matted down from wearing my bike helmet. What kind of wedding attire is this? I definitely won't make it on the front cover of *Bride* magazine.

Kathy, SHED that thought; you've always been unconventional. Why can't you get married in your bike clothes? I looked down at Ron again. He was wearing the exact bright SHED NOW green T-shirt. We loved to bike in our matching outfits, so why not get married in them?

So . . . the minister and I sat by the side of Ron's bed, and he performed the ceremony.

What about rings? Here they are—my parents' rings. The minister began the service. "We are gathered here today . . . "

With a slow, slurred voice Ron repeated what the minister said, "I take Kathy to be my wife . . . till death do us part (Ron added) *and beyond!*"

The minister started to hum the wedding processional. I said, "Stop!" I ran over to the synthesizer on the other side of the bed. (Ron loves music. So, we have musical instruments all over the room.) I said, "Ron, help me . . . what's the chord progression to the wedding march?" In less than a minute, we had it down!

Then, we poured a bottle of water into plastic cups and toasted our marriage! With joyful tears flowing and my mind flashing back to all the wonderful precious memories, I said, "Sweetheart, I am so grateful. Thanks for an amazing five years!"

He responded back, "Yes, and the next five years are going to be even more amazing!" The tears flowed like a Maui waterfall.

I know what you must be thinking. Who gets married *after* their funeral? I did.

The hospice honeymoon was a bit unusual, but my heart was full of *joy*.

Ron passed away three days later.

My grief journey was rough. I cried more the first year than I did all the other years of my life combined. Ron made me promise to write the kids' book on shedding on his deathbed. For years, he had said, "Kathy, you need to start earlier and help kids learn how to SHED." So, I spent three months researching, holding focus groups with kids, and writing the book, *Dealing with Hurt*.

I decided I needed to heal. So, with my doctor's support, I took a three-month sabbatical, moved to Sedona, rented a cabin in the woods on a creek, and took care of two sheep, Wooly and Bully. I became a shepherd. I had someone on my team answer all my emails, and pay all my bills, business and personal, and my cell phone didn't even get reception, so I was fully immersed in this healing grief journey. It was the best gift I've ever given myself.

I slept, I hiked, I sat by the water, I fed my sheep, and I wrote forty thousand words in the book of Ron and my journey.

Finally, in 2020, with the help of a successful Hollywood producer, the screenplay is done!

I still grieve now, but not as intense as the first year or two. And when a grief wave comes, I feel it, bless it, then thank God for it. Then, I let it go. Grief is a sign of how much you loved, and I believe it continues forever in different and sometimes unexpected ways.

My biggest challenge is grieving all the plans we had ahead that we never were able to fulfill, missing my best friend, and laughing until my stomach hurt.

I met Naomi in 1998 at my first National Speakers Association Annual Convention in Philadelphia. She calls me the daughter of her heart, and she was with me every step of this painful journey. God bless her. She sent me an email saying she was starting a support group for widows and gave me the date and time. I responded, "Great! I'd love to be there!" Then, I realized she never intended to invite me to be a part of this group after she responded, "Of course, you should be in this group. Ron died, and you were married for three days." So, instead of a "wedding crasher," I kind of feel like a "widow crasher." But being in this group was providence.

Unlike many who had recently lost their husbands, Ron had passed seven years when I started the group, so I was well on my grief journey. Despite the years, some days, some holidays are still hard and hit me unexpectedly. I also feel I was able to provide some insights, support, and hope to others who were still fresh in their grief.

My favorite week was focused on grief and gratitude because it's important to carry both and not let one fully overtake the other as stated in the Francis Weller quote below.

> *"Gratitude helps us embrace our grief to use it as fuel to propel us forward in our healing."*

God Is Sovereign All the Time

Safe Strong Place (God)
Naomi

I.

Good morning, dear ones!

We look to the Psalms so often when we are hurting, concerned, or needing guidance.

God calls each of us to be "leaders" every day of our lives, with our colleagues, family, and friends. In this time of uncertainty, I turned to the Psalms.

> *Vv. 165 "Great peace have those who love your law,
> and nothing can make them stumble. . . ."*

Stay Balanced

> *Vv. 171–173 "May my lips overflow with praise. May my tongue
> sing of your word, for all your commands are righteous. May
> your hand be ready to help me, for I have chosen your precepts."*

Leaders cannot show the way until they know the way. His way.

. . . so be blessed (we are) . . . even in grief (vv. 1–2)

. . . remain pure and ethical (vv. 9–11)

. . . be strengthened and revitalized (vv. 28, 149, 154–159)

. . . gain wise counsel with need (v. 66)

. . . remain steady, even when afflicted, sad (vv. 67–72, 92)

. . . have a reliable guide even for new issues (vv. 129, 160)

. . . enjoy inward peace and poise (v. 165

. . . get Divine help (vv. 173-175)

II.

Our theme this week is "Gratitude and Grief."

How do we balance the two?

How did Jesus do that?

Jesus wept at the tomb of Lazarus! Why? He knew he was going to raise him from the dead!

He wept at the deep sorrow that Martha and Mary were feeling.

Jesus weeps with you . . . He weeps with me!

Do you think He weeps with you?

Do you think He wept at the funeral/memorial of your spouse?

He also instructs us in gratitude, in praise, "Our Father who art in Heaven, hallowed be thy name. . . "

Picture gratitude and grief on a scale . . . which is over balancing the other right now? this minute, this day, this week?

What is your grief quotient?

What is your gratitude quotient?

Who are you thankful for?

Who can you call or write to today to tell them of your gratitude?

What happens to our grief balance on the scale when we are grateful?

III. Prayer

Dear Lord, comforter of our hearts when we grieve, thank you for *knowing* from *your* Word, and the verification from your spirit, that *you* are Sovereign.

Without that "knowing" . . . it would be so difficult to accept the grief we feel deep inside our hearts for the losses of loved ones.

May we be faithful, now, to share your gospel, the good news of eternity, with *you* . . . so that others may not have to grieve without hope.

Our hope is in *you*, dear Lord! We love you.

Amen.

IV. Questions

1. Are you a person who does well with change, traditionally?

2. Losing a spouse is one of (if not the) most significant changes in life: is it difficult to accept this as part of God's sovereign plan for your life?

3. How do you balance grief and gratitude in facing change?

4. Thanksgiving is coming: contemplate how you can fill your cup with gratitude to balance the grief of a "given" in loss.

5. Are there scriptures that help fill your soul in this "balancing act"?

Marylen's Story

Charles James Veden
May 9, 1936–February 12, 2003
Married 42 years

*And we know that in all things, God works for the good of those
who love him, who have been called according to his purpose.*
Romans 8:28

I lived my early life in Central Minnesota with a family of five. James (Naomi's husband Jim) was my older brother, and Carol, my younger sister. I started school in a rural two-room schoolhouse. James and I were in different rooms, and Mom was his teacher. Our life was middle class and our relationships centered on family and church members. My mom had emigrated from Norway and was "very" Lutheran.

Charles James Veden was born in Wadena, Minnesota May 9, 1936. He was the third Charles, so from his beginning he was known as Jim. We met in Silver Bay, Minnesota in a snow squall in March 1957. I was walking with my best friend, Joyce, and he stopped and asked if he wanted a ride. Joyce and Jim were cousins. A few days later, he asked me for a date. That June, I graduated from high school but went on to the University of Minnesota. In 1959 I took a job at the bank in Silver Bay. Jim worked at the mining company there. We were married in August of 1961. In 1966 we moved to Minneapolis, where we both went to night school at the University of Minnesota. In 1972, we moved to Park Rapids. Our daughter Mary Lynn was born there in 1976.

Jim was a hunter and a fisherman, activities he shared with my father. In my youth I had hunted and fished with my dad and so I did with Jim. In the early years of our marriage, he was a Boy Scout leader and took his troop out camping one weekend a month, even in -40 degree Fahrenheit weather. He earned the Silver Beaver Award and Order of the Arrow.

If God is for us, who can be against us?
Romans 8:31

I had turned in my retirement notice for the end of February 2003. On February 12, Jim said he didn't feel well and had a doctor's appointment. Despite his protests, I went with him. He died of a heart attack on the examining table. We had been married for forty-two and a half years.

I was associated with hospice for many years and facilitated a grief support group. I understood that a grief journey is very personal. I had a group of friends that gathered around me, and we had coffee every Friday. I still attend that group when I'm in the area. With that group, I was able to laugh and cry. Most of them knew

Jim as a friend, so we could tell lots of stories. My family, including James and Naomi, and Carol and Rod, were very good about keeping me on a level "keel." There were invites, and I always felt the family connection.

In Park Rapids, Jim and I were owners/operators of Big Pines RV Park and Campground. It was a dream for Jim, and he did the planning, putting in new sites, maintaining the grounds and buildings, and general fixing. I did the business portion and general office procedures, besides having a forty-hour-a-week job. On May 1, two months after his death, I had to have the park opened for business. Three pumps had to be started to get water to the sites and restrooms. Fourteen acres of land had to be groomed to be a "park." I learned to be a plumber, an electrician, and a groundskeeper. And in the fall, the water lines and pumps had to be emptied and ready for winter.

Jim's aunt, for whom I became the admin after Jim's death, died at the end of March. My mom died the next November, so I was juggling three estates. Each one was very different from the other.

I met Naomi in 1951. I was twelve years old, and she was my brother's girlfriend. Since Naomi was important to him, she was essential to me. In 1957, they were married. James made Naomi my sister, and so it has been. She has been family to me for seventy years, a lifetime. Her children share my DNA.

Naomi knew that I had facilitated grief support groups for Hospice, and she had helped me, as a member of my family, with my grief journey. She told me of the group she wanted to start, and of course, I said yes. I had already met two of the group members on my many visits.

I have been a widow for nineteen years, longer than any in the group. As the journey goes on, I have made the adjustments so that widowhood no longer defines me. I have made a life for myself as a single woman. That does not happen quickly or overnight. This weekly group has helped me grow as a woman of faith and friend. My goal was to help others heal and feel more comfortable with their grief journey. I had many helpers along the way, and I tried to be that helper, reassuring them that God was with them.

> *"For I am convinced that neither death nor life, neither angels nor demons, neither the present nor the future, nor any powers, neither height nor depth, nor anything else in all creation will be able to separate us from the love of God that is in Christ Jesus our Lord." Romans 8:38–39.*

Authentic Labels to Live by

Safe Strong Place (God)
Naomi

I.

Lovely ladies, when I say the word <u>labels</u>, what comes to your mind?

When I say the word *anointed*, what comes to your mind?

II.

God in His sovereign plan has *not* left you to be:

. . . Cloistered

. . . Quiet

. . . Lonely

. . . Without love

. . . Without purpose

Isaiah says we are God's servants, yes, but we are also His anointed leaders. I love that.

And, we have jobs to do:

1. With the infilling Holy Spirit, we enable men and women to fulfill their calls in ministries.

2. We are privileged to "heal the brokenhearted." We have been there ourselves! We know how God comforts!

3. We are to be purveyors of hope and the good news of the Gospel of Jesus Christ.

4. We can undoubtedly comfort those who mourn!

5. We can bring hope and beauty to the lives of those who have lost it!

6. We can set prisoners free . . . lots of people are locked in addictive behavior, etc., that we as anointed ones can help.

7. We can provide happiness and absolute joy that we find in Jesus.

8. We are indeed anointed to tell the good news of His coming again and that He *is* Messiah to our Jewish friends.

> *"The Spirit of the Sovereign Lord is on me because the Lord has anointed me to proclaim the good news to the poor. He has sent me to bind up the brokenhearted, to proclaim freedom for the captives and release from darkness the prisoners, to proclaim the year of the Lord's favor and a day of vengeance of our God to comfort all who mourn, and provide for those who grieve in Zion—to bestow on them a crown of beauty instead of ashes, the oil of joy instead of mourning, and a garment of praise instead of a spirit of despair. They will be called oaks of righteousness, a planting of the Lord for the display of His splendor."*
> *Isaiah 61:1–3 (NIV)*

III. Prayer

Father, we rejoice in your sovereign plan for our lives. Though we are servants, we are also "anointed leaders." Help us to serve with humility and meet the needs of those we intersect with daily.

We love you, Amen.

IV. Questions

1. What comes to your mind when I say the word *labels*? Make a list of labels you have had from a child until now. Wow, long list, right?

2. Was the word *anointed* on your list?

3. "How then shall we live?" (Frances Schaeffer) Perhaps, give thought and writing to how you are fulfilling the "anointing" that God gives for His people in the above Isaiah passage.

4. What "label" would you like to forever erase from your list?

5. What labels would you love to add to your list?

Yes, this takes some thinking, dear ones.

Love you . . . see you next week.

Naomi

Beth Klement

Thomas Vincent Klement, DMD
9/3/1952–8/6/2019 (age 66)
Married 39 years

"But he said to me, 'My grace is sufficient for you,
for my power is made perfect in weakness.'"
2 Corinthians 12:9

While I have been in Naomi's widows' group for almost two years, our friendship dates back to 1985. The common bond that brought me together with Naomi was . . . dentistry! Naomi and her husband Jim were hosting a dental seminar in Maui, Hawaii, and my husband Tom, a dentist, and I were attending. I was instantly drawn to her warm friendliness, enthusiastic faith, and caring wisdom. One afternoon we were relaxing around the pool, getting to know each other, and she asked me how I met my husband.

Tom and I met at the University of Florida in 1979, as I was standing in a long line at the dental school waiting my turn to make an appointment. My eyes glanced down the hall, and I saw my dream guy . . . tall, slender, runner's body, laughing and smiling. I kept looking at him, thinking to myself, *I sure would like to meet him.* Then I noticed he was walking in my direction, and I recognized him . . . he was Tom Klement . . . the shy guy I had gone to junior high and high school with. When he got close enough, he picked up my left hand and asked me if I was married. When I answered, "No, are you?" I thought, *he's not shy anymore,* and asked, "Well, what are you doing Saturday night?" We stood in line, quickly catching up on the nine years since high school graduation.

He helpfully explained the lengthy multi-step intake process for new patients at the dental school.

It didn't sound like I would get a quick answer about the tooth I was concerned about. Tom offered to take a quick look at my mouth right then. At the moment, it seemed like a great way to skip the red tape, and I readily agreed, reminding myself, it helps to know someone. I learned a lot about Tom—he had a personable, calming chairside manner, obviously loved what he did, and was quite good at it. After finishing the quick exam, we stood there in the hallway of the dental school and talked for what seemed to be an hour or more and made plans to go to a play on Saturday night. That day began a lifelong love story with a dentist, but also dentistry—all part of God's sovereign plan and purpose for me.

We dated a couple of times a week and always had so much fun together. But we knew at the end of the summer, he would be going into practice with his older brother Bill in St. Petersburg, and I would be going off to New York to attend Columbia's MBA program. Summer came, Tom graduated and passed his boards and we took a vacation to NYC. Our relationship had grown serious, but neither one of us wanted to ask the other to give up their dreams and alter their plans. One night at a celebratory dinner at The Four Seasons restaurant, over a bottle of champagne, he asked me to marry him. Of course, I said yes! That August, instead of moving to NYC, I moved to St. Petersburg, Florida.

By 1985, Tom was practicing separately from his brother; we had our second daughter and I had quit my job with the Fortune 500 company and decided to return to school to finish my Ph.D. in the fall by commuting to the University of Florida in Gainesville. That summer, Tom and I went to the dental seminar in Maui, Hawaii, conducted by the very popular dental speakers Jim and Naomi Rhode. It would be an excellent combination of vacation and conference. Jim talked about business and marketing, and Naomi talked about team, communication, marriage, and family. And so began my longtime friendship with Naomi!

To say that Naomi made a considerable impact on me is an understatement. I was thirty-three, a mom to two-year-old and seven-month-old daughters. She had a genuine warmth and enthusiasm in meeting and getting to know each person by sharing about herself and asking them questions to get to know them better. I remember sitting by the pool with her one afternoon, and she asked me about my husband, our marriage, and my goals. I shared about going back to school to finish my doctorate.

In August of 1988, I was doing the final edits for my doctoral dissertation on stress in dentists, and my husband's front office team member quit without notice. Tom asked me if I would come in and help him at the office for a week or two until he could find someone else. My first day was Monday, August 8, 1988, our son's two-year-old birthday. That week or two turned into thirty-one years of working together. It wasn't my plan, but it certainly was God's sovereign plan, as together, God combined our gifts and talents to build a practice that now has over sixty employees in two locations and in which three of our four children work as well, two as dentists and one as COO.

Over the next eight years we would go on three more dental seminar vacations with the Rhodes. An Alaskan cruise in 1991, a Virgin Islands cruise in 1993, and a Grecian Isles cruise and trip to Israel in 1996. Jim and Naomi were a beautiful example of a dynamic Christian couple that served others together, and Naomi continued to be a significant influencer in my life.

In the mid-2000s Tom and I went to Phoenix often for dental seminars and would always try to connect with Jim and Naomi over dinner, if they were in town. During one of these dinners in November 2012, Naomi shared that she was no longer speaking since her stroke and instead was doing speech and life coaching. And that is how Naomi became my life coach. We began with weekly calls; she would share quotes and messages and always ask the best, most thought-provoking questions. What is your purpose now? You have maybe twenty more years of real activity; what do you want your legacy to be? How is God working in your life now? How can you deepen your friendship with Tom? What is standing in my way or holding me back? What am I avoiding?

I always took notes and would type them up and send them to her. She listened and helped influence me to be less critical and more optimistic. She modeled for me how to be an encouragement to others. Naomi helped build on the foundation of my Christian faith and trust in God's sovereignty. I memorized one of her favorite sayings, so when hard things happened, I too could say, "Oh well, God is sovereign, and I trust him."

God had been using Naomi to pour into me for three years, with her friendship, mentorship, and coaching to prepare me for what would be the biggest challenge of my life. On Monday afternoon, October 26, Tom went to see the doctor to inquire about his cough that wouldn't go away and the pain in his left side. He called me that afternoon and asked if I could leave work early and come home. They'd done a chest x-ray, which showed a mass in his left lung. When I got in the car to drive home, I was listening to Moody Radio; it was Chris Fabry interviewing Bo Stern, who had been a widow for three weeks. I said, "Lord, is this going to happen to me? Please, no, Lord, don't let this happen to me."

On Wednesday, November 4, 2015, we learned that Tom's diagnosis was stage 4 lung cancer spread to the brain. He'd never been a smoker, hospitalized, or on prescription medicine. His treatment regimen was whole-brain radiation followed by a targeted therapy drug. In two months, he was declining fast, and on January 5, 2016, Tom felt like he was dying; he weighed one hundred pounds and asked me if he had signed everything he needed to sign. Fortunately, I had a call with Naomi that morning, and she coached me through and provided encouragement and inspiration to keep up the good fight. Naomi said we are "one person" and we are stronger together. Every day we are (still) alive is another opportunity to glorify God. We have an opportunity to "straighten up" and not "curl up." That Tom may not know what his purpose is anymore. She shared a Mark Twain quote: "The two most important days in your life are the day you are born and the day you find out why."

Tom was the beneficiary of a medical miracle. He had stared death in the face and did get better. They switched him to another targeted med. He took four pills every morning and every evening. For two and a half years, our life returned to "almost normal." We traveled to places on our bucket list and made three international trips. God gave us a reprieve. Then in November 2018, the cancer progressed to a lymph node in his chest, which pressed on his esophagus and closed it off. He needed to go on a feeding tube and could not even drink water. He couldn't sleep lying flat, as he would wake up choking on his saliva, so he slept propped up on the downstairs couch. They tried various treatments—chemotherapy, radiation, immunotherapy, and one more targeted med. Nothing was stopping the cancer's progression. I knew my biggest fear was coming true . . . I would be a widow. Tom was promoted to heaven on August 6, 2019.

I did not want to be a widow. I did not like the word. I decided if I was going to be one, I wanted to sign up for Grief Share, and over the next sixteen months, I read more than twenty books on grief, thinking perhaps I could get past it sooner. I would learn soon enough that grief does not work that way. There was no accelerated class. It would take time, and it would take work. There would be ups and many downs, and as soon as I thought I was making progress, there would be setbacks. I would learn to move forward, little by little.

My biggest challenge as a widow has been defining who I am now. I am not a wife anymore, yet it's hard to identify myself as single. Where I work is the practice we built together. Now I lead it, yet I liked it better when I was a solid second to Tom. It took me a year to "move in" to his office. It took me seventeen months to be able to clear out his closet, as I had purchased so many of his shirts. What are my goals and my dreams now? I honestly don't know; I am still trying to figure that out. They were so clear before when we decided on them together. When someone at work asked me what I wanted to do for vacation, I cried. I had no idea; I lost my person to do things with. I always liked talking over things with Tom; he was decisive, I am not, and I miss that. Maybe the very hardest part of being a widow is not having Tom to hug me when I need comfort or reassurance, knowing that we can get through whatever the disappointments or challenges are together. Another thing I miss is not having him here to share the family joys—our kids' accomplishments, getting married, buying a house, having a baby.

When I had been a widow for a little more than a year, Naomi asked me to be in the group. I readily said yes, knowing that if Naomi were facilitating it, it would be great. It has been so healing to share our hurts, fears, and struggles with other women who understand the heartache, the loneliness, the tears, and some of the successes too. It has been so encouraging to hear from women who lost their husbands many years ago. It has given me confidence that I too will get there someday with God's help. It's been beneficial to have women who are earlier in the grief process that I can help and encourage and be reminded of God's help in getting me through those early stages of grief.

My favorite week of our widows' group was the day we answered the question about how we met our husbands. The conversation was so happy and lively that each woman glowed as she shared her story of how she met her spouse, and I concluded that love, the love between a husband and wife is a miracle, an absolute miracle of God. The bringing together of two very different individuals, the sacred bonding of marriage, the learning to live together, raising children, being a living, breathing example to others that God created marriage to reflect Him to our hurting world. Although I am no longer married to Tom, I can look back and see how God has grown me through loss; my heart is bigger, my compassion is greater, and my understanding is deeper. I have learned through experience that God truly means what he promises in His word . . . that He will never leave us or forsake us, that He will work all things together for good, that He has plans for me, that He is doing a new thing, that His grace is sufficient and His power is made perfect in my weakness . . . that He is sovereign in all things and I can trust Him.

Jesus Wept Too

Safe Strong Place (God)
Naomi

I.

Twice this week at church, we read that Jesus wept. He wept when Lazarus died. He wept in the garden of Gethsemane over the city of Jerusalem.

He knew . . . He knew what that last week would hold.

He knew how fickle the people would be.

He knew they would soon cry, "Crucify Him, crucify Him." He came humbly on the colt of a donkey, not riding on a horse like a king! Interesting, the word *palm* also relates to the soft part of our hand, and it says in scripture that our "names are written in the palms of His hands." And then the words that ring in our hearts and must also be personalized by us:

> *"Father, forgive them, for they know not what they do."*
> *Luke 23:34*

II.

So, today, I want us to focus on His example of forgiveness.

Forgiveness that they did *not* deserve!

99

Forgiveness that He did not need to extend!

Forgiveness that is a model for us also.

When we do not forgive, we carry that burden on *our* shoulders. It weighs us down and keeps us from the free/loving life that God intended for us.

III. Quotes on Forgiveness

"The weak can never forgive. Forgiveness
is the attribute of the strong."
Mahatma Gandhi

"Resentment is like a glass of poison that a man drinks.
Then he sits down and waits for his enemy to die."
Nelson Mandela

"Forgiveness is the key which unlocks the door of
resentment and the handcuffs of hatred. It breaks the
chains of bitterness and the shackles of selfishness."
Corrie Ten Boom

IV. Prayer

Oh, Father, you tell us in your Word the power of forgiveness.

You show us on the cross the *power* of *forgive*ness.

You model for us as followers of *your* will and *your* way.

We ask for both the remembrance and the desire to forgive those in our past that may still linger in the fiber of our souls to cause self-destructive patterns in our present lives.

May we know that the only *true forgiveness* is forgiveness that is empowered by your spirit.

We need your help, Lord . . . we want to be women of forgiveness, and the peace and power that resides in our hearts that are clean from that baggage. In your precious name, Amen. Indeed!

Amen and Amen.

V. Questions

1. Has there ever been a time when it was very difficult for you to forgive?

2. Has there ever been a time when it was tough to believe that He could forgive you? Share.

3. Share how you met your spouse.

4. What did you love most about your spouse?

5. Share one of the happy times you had together.

6. Share one of the most challenging times together.

Judy Huber

Husband: Ron Huber
September 24, 1945–October 29, 2004
Married 39 years

---

*"The widow who is really in need and left all
alone puts her hope in God and continues night
and day to pray and to ask God for help."*
I Timothy 5:5

My husband and I were married for thirty-nine years; we have two married daughters and seven grandchildren. We started a business together in 1978, and my husband had a personal goal to retire by the time he was fifty years old. He did it! We sold our company in 1995, just five months before he had his fiftieth birthday and retired. After his retirement, we traveled and enjoyed our grandchildren and each other. He became a little "restless" and started another fun business for him, and I continued to remain "retired."

Life was good. My husband started another business that included his passion for racing and cars. We had a small car collection, and he restored vintage Nascars and was in a Vintage Nascar Racing group along with a new business of importing Tony Kart Go-Karts from Italy. All this did not include me being an integral part of the business, which was more than fine with me.

I was thrilled to be spending time with the grands, and we had a home in Flagstaff, Arizona, to enjoy with the family in the summers.

He had just received his first shipment of the go-karts to our warehouse and was heading to Las Vegas, Nevada, for the National Go-Kart Race with racers coming from all over the US. It was a fascinating time. On Thursday morning of that race week, I got a call from the race manager that Ron had had an accident while riding his Segway and was unconscious. An ambulance had been called. While I was concerned, for sure, this was not the first time he had "hit his head," and he had always bounced right back up. I told the race manager to call me back if he had not come around when the ambulance arrived, and I was wondering just what to do. I was in Scottsdale, Arizona, and knew that if I went to Las Vegas to be with him, I would find him sitting up in bed at the hospital eating Jell-O and him telling me I didn't need to have come. When the phone rang the second time, just shortly after we had hung up, I knew in my heart that all was not well. I spoke to the EMT, and she asked me about any medication he was on. I could hear in the background the other EMT trying to wake Ron up. He did not regain consciousness and did not survive his head injury. Ron passed away the following evening, October 29, 2004.

My life changed "in a heartbeat."

My grief journey began that Thursday afternoon when I arrived in Las Vegas, Nevada, with my two daughters and brother. My brother had driven up from Southern California to be with us, and we all arrived at the hospital in Las Vegas within minutes of one another.

I asked to see Ron and was told I had to speak with the doctor before visiting my husband. And so, it began.

In the beginning, I didn't have time to think about "grief." I was heartbroken, and many tears were shed, but there were so many things that needed to be done during the first two weeks that there was no time to grieve. My friends and family surrounded me with love and care. After everyone was gone and I was alone, the grief process began.

My daughters and I went to grief counseling together at our church, and we learned a lot about grief, and one thing that stood out to me was that they told us to "tell our story to those that asked and wanted to know what had happened." I did that and still do now, seventeen years later, not as often as in the beginning, but a few times here and there. What that did for me was to accept the finalization of his death and that no, he was not on another business trip and no, this time, he would not be coming home.

Those were hard days for me. I was fifty-eight years old. According to the "stats," I knew most likely that my husband would pass away before me, and I would probably be a widow. But this was too soon; Ron was only fifty-nine years old and gone way too early. I did not want to be a widow, and I didn't want to be a member of the Widows' Bible Study at church. I still don't like the word "widow"! I was angry; how could this happen to me? I was angry at my husband for leaving me, I felt abandoned, and I lost my self-confidence; I wondered, "So who am I now if I am not Mrs. Judy Huber, wife of Ron Huber?" I had my two daughters grieving for their father and six grandchildren grieving for their Papa; it was overwhelming. The only thing I could do was call out to God for His help, His guidance, and His words of comfort so that I could share that comfort with my family.

I have been a Christian since I was eighteen years old, but I must admit, I did not know how much God loved me until this time in my life. I had lost my father a few years before Ron passed away, and that was so hard, but God got me through that, and He was there for me now, every step of the way; I just had to reach out to Him and give my burden to Him and let Him guide me. And finally, the most important question of all for me was when I asked God, "Okay, Lord, what would you have me do with my life now?" I needed to put my life in the hands of my heavenly Father and follow Him as He guided my path and my life going forward.

Grief is interesting. It gets better as the years go by, but there are times, out of the blue, that it rears its ugly head again, and it feels like it was just yesterday that Ron passed away, and for a moment, I can fall back into the "pit."

I am so grateful that God has brought me through all of this and my life has certainly changed from how I imagined it would be now, but I have a precious gift that God has given me, and that is "contentment." I am content with my life, and there is joy in my life again. God is so good!

So, do you remember that part about my husband starting "a new business of importing Tony Kart Go-Karts from Italy"? God has such a funny sense of humor. Two weeks after Ron's death, I went down to the warehouse to announce to the four employees that I was closing the business. Boy, did that change. The office part of the warehouse was in the front, and when I opened the door to the warehouse part of the building, it was ten thousand square feet of go-karts stacked in boxes about ten feet high and as far as you could see, plus vintage Nascar racing cars, engines for the race cars, a Hotrod or two, and a huge motorhome. I remember slamming the door to the warehouse and telling our sweet assistant, "I am so mad at Ron right now; how could he do this to me?" To which she replied, "I'm mad at him too."

I ran a woman-owned go-kart business for two years after Ron passed away. I was the only female importer of go-karts in the US. I had a racing team of twenty-five kids and young men. I traveled to all the races to support our team. We were featured in all the go-kart magazines. Our race team finished first in multiple categories, and I sold a lot of go-karts and increased our go-kart distributors from six to thirty-five across the US. This is not what I had planned for my life, and I often ask God, "Really, Lord?"

That, by far, was my biggest challenge as a widow. Not my dream, not my kind of business; I knew nothing about go-karts and did not want to do this! There were lots of tears shed, and my husband's loss was amplified daily. I would say, "So, what would Ron do?" All I can say is that God was at work, restoring my confidence, soul, faith, strength, and love for my God. It was a fantastic time of personal growth in every way possible.

Naomi Rhode and I knew of one another for some time, we attended the same church together for a short while, and they were customers of ours from our earlier business. (Not the go-kart part. . .) For the last five or six years, Naomi has been a committee member of a committee I chaired at Phoenix Seminary called Women of Momentum. We have a Women of Momentum Scholarship Fund, and we raise funds for that scholarship, providing scholarships for the female students at the seminary. Our friendship has grown over these past years. She is an amazing woman and loves the Lord. I am so blessed to have her in my life.

Naomi called me and shared her plan to put a group together of women that she knew, some were newly widowed, and she thought my experience as a widow for seventeen years could help the group. I immediately said yes and saw this as a way I could help other women through my experience as a widow.

In the beginning, I came to the group to be of help to these ladies which I did not know, and many of these ladies did not know one another. But I must admit, these ladies are amazing women, and they have helped me more than I have helped them. I wanted to be there for them. I have gone through my "widowhood" without someone around to cheer me on. So, I have realized that everything they are experiencing, I experienced and that the feelings I had are normal, and it is all a process that we all will go through as widows. It has shown me the importance of having a support group around you and continues to demonstrate the love of the Lord Jesus Christ for us and that we should always be in the business of women helping women.

Every time we meet is fantastic, but this particular morning, Monday, January 28, 2022, challenged me in a big way. You see, I moved in June 2022 to a different home. I downsized again. I did it once before and I didn't like it then, and I'm not crazy about it now. The actual move was rough in too many ways to mention. It was not what I wanted to do. The market was strong, and it was an excellent time to sell; I understood all the reasons for a move in my head, but my head and my heart were not in sync.

So, as I listened to the discussion of creating an "Ebenezer" to commemorate what God has done in my life, I thought, hmm, *I am grateful for all that God has done in my life; why am I not feeling that gratefulness in my heart for this house?* I know this is where God wants me; it was made pretty clear. I read the notes in our discussion, "Have you ever created an Ebenezer? Have you thought of the gifts from God that he has bestowed on you? And do you realize that God is our comfort and our provider? Jehovah Jireh: The Lord will provide! Amen."

The next couple of days, I was outside planting some spring flowers, and to my surprise, there was a little stack of rocks just to the left of my driveway and I went, *hmm,* so I started gathering a few more stones and managed to build an Ebenezer!

So, it is right there, and I see it every time I drive into my driveway, and I always say, "Thank you, Lord, for your provision, and I'm celebrating what you have done in my life, and thank you, Lord, for providing this home for me." It has changed my heart, and this house is becoming more like home every day! I am so grateful! Praise God for His goodness and mercy; thank you, Jesus.

Rock Collecting

Safe Strong Place (God)
Naomi

I.

Dear ones, time to collect some rocks!

I just finished studying the book of Nehemiah . . . *great* book, *great leader*!

Nehemiah saw a job that needed to be done . . . the people were back in Israel . . . and the wall was in shambles and needed to be rebuilt!

Wow, they did it! And then they celebrated!

II.

Perhaps in our losses in life, we do not stop celebrating the:

1. Gains

2. Goodness

3. Grace

4. *Gratitude*

Celebrations can occur in many ways, but one of the ways that Nehemiah and the people celebrated was to create: *Ebenezer's stones of help!*

> *"Then Samuel took a stone and set it up between*
> *Mizpah and Shen. He named it Ebenezer, saying,*
> *'Thus far the Lord has helped us.'"*
> *I Samuel 7:12*

Remembering and reflecting on the good things in life helps you to navigate during the hard times, perhaps even through "divine distance."

III.

So . . . let's do some collecting:

Providential Rocks of Remembrance!

(Let's collect some rocks!)

Rocks from the battlefield of life commemorating what God has done in my life!

Rocks to celebrate spirituality and selationality!

IV. Prayer

Father, how wondrous to imagine the Ebenezers that have been built to honor the remembrance of your faithfulness. We have many of those in our memories, Lord. Help us to occasionally build or help someone else make an actual Ebenezer. Oh . . . and another thought, Lord: may our wedding rings be Ebenezers of the faithfulness of those shared years together and with you. We love you, and thank you for your goodness daily in our lives, Amen.

V. Questions

1. Have you ever created an Ebenezer? (Maybe a literal stone you placed somewhere.)

2. Do you have something in your home that is an Ebenezer, perhaps a piece of jewelry?

3. Have you thought of the list of your Ebenezers as gifts from God for your growth in Him?

4. Might you want to do a remembrance like this with a family member, a friend, or by yourself? When?

5. Do you, do I realize that God's provision is always in our lives, daily and that He is our comfort and our provider?

6. Jehovah Jireh means "the Lord will provide." Amen.

Now What?

SAFE STRONG PLACE (GOD)
Naomi

I.

Precious readers, and that you are!

You have taken the time to read stories of what other remarkable widows have experienced.

You have read some of the fifty-three weekly Zoom sessions that we have shared. The rest are included with the holidays at the end.

You have felt our hearts of listening to each other, loving each other, and encouraging each other to remember that our God is a sovereign God.

Our God loves us, and He will comfort and care for us in our significant losses.

You have walked with us through the grief journey, finding new paths of recovery and purpose with God as our heavenly husband.

One of my favorite quotes from Frances Schaeffer is, "How then shall we live?"

So, my question to you, dear reader, as you put this book down, for now, is:

"How then should *you* live?"

How has this book changed your view of losing a spouse?

How has this book opened your heart to reach out and love those who have suffered a loss?

How has this book, *perhaps*, caused you to want to start a group yourself?

If so . . . ask God to recall those who are widowed or divorced in your life, friends whom you know, and who you care deeply about in their loss.

With the wonder of Zoom, these friends can be located all over the country.

(That may even be best, as vulnerability is critical.)

I would love for you to accept this challenge.

II.

Recipe for starting a group:

1. The word of God and His presence in your lives!

2. A facilitator (does not need to be widowed or divorced. I was the facilitator, and I am not widowed/divorced)

3. Seven to nine people is the best if you have a one-hour meeting.

4. Send them an invitation to be part of this group, setting the time and day of the week you will be meeting.

5. Have a Zoom account or have one of the women in your group manage the Zoom link and the recording link, and send sessions to those who cannot attend for some reason. (Delightfully, we have had almost perfect attendance for a year and a half, every week, for one hour.)

6. Choose a theme for each week, e.g., seasons, does grief dissipate/change, forgiveness, or grief affecting extended family members, etc.

7. As a leader, take five to nine minutes to share your ideas on the theme—any references, quotes, etc.

8. Send out your written plan for each day, with questions addressing the theme several days before the Zoom call.

9. After starting each call with your thoughts on the theme, call on each member to share answers to the questions as God moves them. Welcome Q&A about the theme also.

10. Consider having an annual two- or three-day retreat in a hotel or resort.

11. Let me know if you have started a group! You are welcome to use all the material in this book as templates for your beginnings.

To God be the glory!

Blessings, Naomi

We're Not Dead, He's Not Done

I.

Good morning, dear ones that I love!

II.

Here is a verse for you to ponder.

> *"And the LORD blessed the latter days of Job more than*
> *his beginning. And he had 14,000 sheep, 6,000 camels,*
> *1,000 yoke of oxen, and 1,000 female donkeys."*
> *Job 42:12 (ESV)*

Wow, wow, wow!

Remember, this is after:

Loss of his family

Loss of his entire fortune

Loss of friends who would stand by him

114

Loss of his health; he was covered with sores!

Conclusion: life is over or is it?

Oh, no . . . No, no . . . No!

The rest of his life was just beginning

The rest of his life was restored because of his faithfulness to God:

1. Children were restored.

2. His fortune was restored.

3. His purpose and promise were restored.

When did you read the whole book of Job last? It is a very long book.

Will this suffering ever *end?* Will the ridicule from friends ever *end?*

It did, but God does not end!

III.

Job 33:19–29 says:

> *"Man is also rebuked with pain on his bed and with continual strife in his bones so that his life loathes bread and his appetite the choicest food. His flesh is so wasted away that it cannot be seen, and his bones that were not seen stick out. His soul draws near the pit, and his life to those who bring death. If there be for him an angel, a mediator, one of the thousand, to declare to man what is right for him, and he is merciful to him, and says, 'Deliver him from going down into the pit; I have found a ransom; let his flesh become fresh with youth; let him return to the days of his youthful vigor;' then man prays to God, and he accepts Him; He sees his face with a shout of joy and restores to man his righteousness. He sings before men and says: 'I sinned and perverted what is*

right, and it was not repaid to me. He has redeemed my soul from
going down into the pit, and my life shall look upon the light.'
Behold, God does all these things, twice, three times,
with a man, to bring back his soul from the pit, and
that he may be lighted with the light of life.

When Job saw his sores close up and heal, he chose to
get up from his sickbed. When he realized his sorrow was
not the end, he chose to eat again. When he discovered
the goodness of God even in tragedy, he decided to
keep living so God would have a life to bless."

IV.

After any storm, there is time spent assessing the damage. Time
to realize what was lost and what remains. I don't know what you
may have lost due to life's unexpected storms: a loved one, a cherished relationship, or the comfort of what used to be. What I do
know is that if you're reading this, you still have life for God to
bless. That life may be different, but with God, it can still be good.
God still has a plan for you.

VI.

Job teaches us not to allow our fear of getting knocked down to
overtake our faith to keep getting back up. There is life on the
other side of loss, and God is able to bless it.

VII. Prayer

"Dear Heavenly Father, thank you for being with me
through every storm I face. As I navigate life after loss, I
pray that your love restores my hope and that Your strength
empowers me to keep living. In Jesus' Name, Amen."
—Christina Patterson

VIII. QUESTIONS

1. What do you think of first when you read the above?

2. If the tragedy of losing your spouse was a 10 on a scale of 1–10, where does that loss rate today?

3. Write a "Job list" of what you have lost in all of life! Every kind of loss!

4. Write a "self-list" of all you have been blessed with in life!

5. What is your conclusion?

6. Frances Shaffer asks, "How then shall we live?"

7. What is next?

What about Divorce?

A Safe, Strong Place
Naomi

I.

Good morning, dear ones!

1 Thessalonians: 5:18 says:

> *"Give thanks in all circumstances, for this is the will of God for you in Christ Jesus."*

Wow, *all* circumstances!

Give thanks for His:

Protection

Provision

Presence

II.

A quote from Paul Tripp that I love (if I have shared it before, this is a great review and time to maybe memorize it) says:

"If you are God's child, you are loved today, even if, in your human relationships, you are or you feel completely alone."

In other words, as believers, we are *never alone!*

Amazing grace!

> *"I am nearer than you dare believe, closer*
> *than the air you breathe."*
> *Psalm 94*

> *"If my children could only recognize my presence,*
> *they would never feel lonely again."*
> *"For this and much more, we are thankful!"*
> *Sarah Young*

Prayer for our precious time . . .

III.

We have an excellent guest today. He is a very dear friend.

Dr. John Pefferle came to one of our seminars when he was just out of Dental School. John has had a very successful Children's Dental Practice in Raleigh, North Carolina. But the important thing is the massive change in his life when he turned his life over to the Lord. John is not a widower, he is divorced, and his experience causes us to understand how our ministry to widows should also apply to those who suffer a divorce. We don't note and reach out to care for people when divorce happens or a former spouse dies like we do when a current spouse dies, but they are similar losses.

IV. Prayer

Father, we come to you with questions. We ask "why," and your answer often is "wait"! You want us to wait to see your full glory, Father, in even the hardest of situations! And we are not alone in the waiting. Your Holy Spirit encourages us, comforts us, holds us. We shall behold the reasons "why" . . . we are "waiting," Lord! Amen!

IV. Questions

1. How do you think the pain of divorce (a spouse choosing to leave you) differs from the death of a spouse?

2. What have been your most effective means of not just surviving but thriving?

3. Are you personally ever lonely?

4. How do you handle loneliness?

5. What can we learn from what you have learned about the Body of Christ? How do we care for each other through sad times, or how do we miss the opportunity?

6. What do you wish I would ask you right now?

Widowhood

Safe Strong Place (God)
Naomi

I.

It has been a rainy, gloomy day, all day today, the day I wrote this to you. This almost *never* happens in Phoenix.

I vacillate between a cozy afghan, making chicken soup with Jim, and *even* making bread for the first time in years from scratch. Why do I have a feeling of hunkering down, a sense of being a tad "blue"?

And then . . .

II.

Psalm 143:8 comes alive in my soul as David writes:

> *"Listen to my plea; I am losing hope, I am paralyzed with fear; I reach out for you. I thirst for you. Come quickly, Lord, and answer me, for my depression deepens. Let me hear of your unfailing love to me."*

Wow! David is paralyzed with fear? Have you ever been there?

We probably can all identify, certainly, when standing before a casket of our beloved!

David does not read a self-help book. *He turns to God alone!*

"Show me where to walk, for I have come to you in prayer. Teach me to do your will. May your gracious Spirit lead me forward on to firm footing. For the glory of your name, O Lord, save me. In your righteousness, bring me out of this distress. In your unfailing love, cut off all my enemies. . . . For I am your servant."
Psalm 143:10–12

David *knew* of His love. He blessed His name and *believed!*

Time to praise Him for His salvation, His unfailing love, His sovereign plan for our lives, His Spirit, which indwells and empowers us.

He forgave all our sins and intercedes for us right now before the throne of God in heaven. Wow!

Amen!

III. Prayer

Father, precious Father, we so often flinch at the word "widowhood" and all it stands for . . . grief, loneliness, sadness, loss. We are comforted by much—family, friends, the church, and your word. Often you recognize us in your word, and you ask the Body of Christ to care for us, to be cognizant of our needs. Thank you, Lord, and thank you for the model of care you give us, even from the cross, where you, as your beloved John, care for your mother. And, we know from history, Lord, that he did! Thank you for knowing our deepest needs . . . we love you, Amen.

IV. Questions

1. What are you thinking as you read the above?

2. When is this most applicable for you?

3. What do you tend to do when you are "down"?

4. Do you call someone? Who hears your tears?

5. Do you believe in His *unfailing love* for you? How do you experience that?

I just received this . . . thought it was good

Widow.

At first, I hated the word; after all, I'm too young to be a widow! But scripture reminds me that widows are very precious to God, and I cannot despise what He loves, even when it's me.

Lately, I've been pondering what it means to be a widow. How can I even describe it? It's so much . . . and yet, so much nothing at the same time.

Last night, another pastor's widow sent this to me, and although I didn't write it, I feel every word so deeply. So, if you want a peek inside the mind and heart of a widow, keep reading. Then say a prayer for every precious widow and widower in your life. It was written by Alisha Bozart and is available on her website:

> *Widowhood is more than missing your spouse's presence. It is adjusting to an alternate life. It is growing around a permanent amputation.*
> *Widowhood is going to bed for the thousandth time, and still, the loneliness doesn't feel normal. The empty bed a constant reminder. The night no longer brings intimacy and comfort but the loudness of silence and the void of connection.*
> *Widowhood is walking around the same house you have lived in for years, and it no longer feeling like home. Because "home"*

incorporated a person. And they're not there. Homesickness fills your heart and the knowledge that it will never return haunts you. Widowhood is seeing all your dreams and plans you shared as a couple crumble around you. The painful process of searching for new dreams that include only you amount to climbing Mount Everest. And every small victory of creating new dreams for yourself includes a new shade of grief that their death propelled you to this path.

Widowhood is second-guessing everything you thought you knew about yourself. Your life had molded together with another's, and without them, you have to relearn all your likes, hobbies, fears, goals. The renaissance of a new person makes you proud and heart-broken simultaneously.

Widowhood is being a stranger in your own life. The unnerving feeling of watching yourself from outside your body, going through the motions of what was your life, but being detached from all of it. You don't recognize yourself. Your previous life feels but a vapor long gone, like a mist of a dream you begin to wonder if it happened at all. Widowhood is the irony of knowing if that one person was here to be your support, you would have the strength to grieve that one person. The thought twists and confuses you. If only they were here to hold you and talk to you, you'd have the tenacity to tackle this unwanted life. To tackle the arduous task of moving on without them.

Widowhood is missing the one person who could truly understand what is in your heart to share. The funny joke, the embarrassing incident, the fear compelling you, or the frustration tempting you. To anyone else, you would have to explain, and that is too much effort, so you keep it to yourself. And loneliness grows inside you.

Widowhood is struggling with identity. Who are you if not their spouse? What do you want to do if not the things you planned together? What brand do you want to buy if not the one you two shared for twenty years? What is your purpose if the job of investing into your marriage is taken away? Who is my closest companion when my other half isn't here?

Widowhood is feeling restless because you lost your home, identity, partner, lover, friend, playmate, travel companion, co-parent, security, and life. And you are drifting with an unknown destination.

Widowhood is living in a constant state of missing the most intimate relationship. No hand to hold. Nobody is next to you. No partner to share your burden.

Widowhood is being alone in a crowd of people. Feeling sad even while you're happy. Feeling guilty while you live. It is looking back while moving forward. It is being hungry but nothing sounds good. It is every special event turning bittersweet.

Yes. It is much more than simply missing their presence. It is becoming a new person, whether you want to or not. It is fighting every emotion mankind can feel at the very same moment and trying to function in life at the same time.

Widowhood is frailty. Widowhood is strength. Widowhood is darkness. Widowhood is rebirth.

Widowhood. . . .is life changing.

From Alisha Bozarth at alishabozarth.com

We Owe God Everything

Safe Strong Place (God)
Naomi

I.

Good morning, dear ones!

Naomi Catchup for those who know and love us—hopefully that is all of you!

We had five college guys who flew in from Louisville to celebrate our grandson's birthday . . . all six stayed at our house, so we went to Sedona for a few days. *Great* idea. Washed over twenty pool towels, loads of sheets, etc. They *left* five half gallons of ice cream. Shucks, we will have to eat that. So thrilled they could enjoy our home, pool, hot tub, cabana, etc.

Then, the inevitable happened. Our landlord, after five and a half years, said, "We do not know how to ask our parents to leave." They think of us that way, but they want to move back into this home, completely redo it, and retire here. So, we need to move; they want it as soon as we find a place. Wisdom needed!

Oh, and I have started a gratitude journal as I suggested you do. Five things every morning for the previous day. It is extraordinary and you are on this list for today, big time! I love you all so much.

I am anxious to hear your hearts and what the Lord was doing already in your life this year!

II.

Verse for today. It is a perfect one:

> *"His divine power has given us everything we need*
> *for life and Godliness through our knowledge of Him*
> *who called us by His own glory and goodness."*
> *2 Peter 1:3*

Wow . . . all we need . . . and we are called!

Let's revel in gratitude for that reality!

III. Prayer

Oh, Father, how grateful we are for the gift of hospitality. Sometimes we feel that we are not able to provide proper hospitality because we are limited by our circumstances or the home we live in. Or are we? We *really* dwell in your arms of care and love and the "house" we reside in is somewhat optional. Thank you for that assurance, as our circumstances change because we lost our husbands, we need that assurance! With huge blessings, sometimes, you send trials, *and* supply the wisdom to move forward. Thank you, Amen.

V. Questions

1. Have you thought of starting a gratitude journal?

2. Have you thought of calling one hundred people this year . . . just to touch base . . . maybe pulling a different Christmas card from 2020 each day to pray for that family, and perhaps contact them?

3. It says in the Welcoming Prayer, "All our feelings are gifts and teachers. They are not enemies we need to avoid."

4. What are prominent "feelings" you had?

5. Did you welcome them or "fight them"?

6. Did you learn from them?

7. Where are the "holy places" you worship most?

Surrender

Safe Strong Place (God)
Naomi

I.

Good morning, precious friends!

It has been a very disruptive week in my life. This is 2021, and I am concerned for our country, concerned for Covid's side effects on our society, concerned for you and the profound losses in your life, and our necessary move.

Then . . . I received a poem I want to share with you . . . and a song I want you to listen to . . . all the way through . . . to bring a calm and peace to your spirit as it has to mine:

> *"May you know that absence is alive*
> *With hidden presence,*
> *That nothing is ever lost or forgotten.*
> *May the absences in your life*
> *Grow full of eternal echo.*
> *May you sense around you the secret*
> *Elsewhere, where the presences*
> *That have left you dwell.*
> *May you be generous*
>
> *In your embrace of loss.*
> *May the sore well of grief turn into*

> *A seamless flow of presence.*
> *May you be embraced by God,*
> *In Whom dawn and twilight are one*
> *Within the Great Belonging. "*
> *A Blessing for Absence, from Littlefootprints.org.uk*

II.

Now . . . the topic that we are looking at today is *surrender.*

Before you answer the questions . . . I want to share some thoughts:

1. The why of surrender: God's will for our lives . . . and it brings *peace.*

2. Surrender is *not* an event . . . it is a "way of life," and the result is not only peace but "the fruit of righteousness."

3. Elizabeth Elliot's example: She took Valerie into the jungle with the Auca Tribe, who killed her father and the other four missionary men.

4. We are to surrender to the Word of God.

5. Our first surrender . . . when we come to Christ . . . for salvation.

6. Surrender . . . Trusting God . . . (my main word for the year is *trust*)

III. Prayer

Dear Lord, I surrender all to you today . . . my heart, my body, and my soul. Please help me to eliminate the fears that stand in my way. Please take charge of my life and give me the peace of living in your almighty will. Amen.

IV. Questions

1. How would you, as a believer, define *surrender?*

2. Are there scriptures that support and example surrender?

3. How important is it in our lives as Christians?

4. What are examples of surrender since your husband went to heaven?

5. When you surrender, how does it make you feel?

"Submit yourselves, then go to God. Resist
the devil, and he will flee from you."
James 4:7

1. When you resist surrendering . . . how does it make you feel?

2. I asked a friend her thoughts on *surrender*. . . and she shared this profound thought: "God is always trying to give good things to us, but our hands can be too full." Hmmm . . . that spoke to my experience . . . and certainly how I feel about having to move.

3. How about you?

4. How could we be closer in our relationship with each other's thoughts?

Shedding

Safe Strong Place (God)
Naomi

---

*"To everything there is a season, and a time
to every purpose under heaven."*
Ecclesiastes 3:1

I.

Good morning, dear ones,

It has been a rain-soaked week in Arizona . . . *lots* of snow in the mountains, if you want to come and go skiing. There is even a tiny bit of snow on some of the cars this early morning.

Amazing what can happen in a week's time . . .

Do you ever feel like the "Queen of Shedding"? (By the way, congratulations to our resident author Kathy, she got the rights to the word *SHED* . . . so we have to pay her every time we use it, haha!)

Well . . . I feel like the queen . . . got my crown this week . . . the crown of shedding.

We have been looking for houses to lease, and finally, the two top of the list . . . amazing/beautiful/incredible homes up on the mountain; we were OK'd for today. And *then* . . . our daughter says, "Mom/Dad . . . there is a house to lease around the corner, and one block from us . . . please consider it . . . we want to be 'here' for you . . . not thirty minutes away if you need us. You *are* getting older."

I had not noticed that . . . so I ran to the mirror, and I did have some wrinkles . . . just barely starting . . . and Jim announced, "*Finally*, Naomi . . . you are starting to have a sixty-year-old face!"

So, we are going to lease it . . . *not* in the neighborhood I would have chosen, or the house I would have chosen, but the neighbors have been chosen for us . . . by our sovereign God . . . the same day!

Why am I sharing my "shedding" minutia? Well . . . we will considerably have to downsize. We spent six man-hours (three each) packing half my books the last night. I sorted them into boxes for the library to take, etc., etc.). I have to get rid of a lot of clothes! Let me know if you need some!

I am sharing because . . .

We *all* are shedding all the time . . . life is all about "change."

You may be saying, "Tell me about it!" Most of you had to shed a closet full of your husband's clothes . . . maybe all of you have done that . . . that has to be the hardest thing in the world to shed.

I remember as a child, we were moving from Minnesota to Arizona, and my mother burned the box of letters that she had written to my dad . . . the love letters. I saw my dad put his head down on the banister and cry. I was in seventh grade . . . and obviously have not forgotten.

II. Prayer

Dear Lord, please allow me to let go of the fears and baggage of life that I cling to. Please cleanse my heart and my mind of all things that keep me from focusing on your word. Please help me to turn my eyes only on you and submit only to you. Amen.

III. Questions

1. What have you had to shed since your husband died?

2. What are you still shedding?

3. Looking to the future, what will you still need to shed as you grow older without your spouse?

4. Are there others in your life that are encouraging you to shed?

5. What emotions do you need to shed?

Words

Safe Strong Place (God)
Naomi

I.

Good morning, beautiful ladies that I love.

II.

Bible verse for today:

> *"Oh, that we might know the Lord.*
> *Let us press on to know Him.*
> *He will respond to us as surely as the arrival of dawn*
> *Or the coming of rains in early spring."*
> *Hosea 6:3*

Love that!

> *"The Lord will do amazing things among you."*
> *Joshua 3:5*

Moses died on Mt. Nebo after blessing Joshua to take over and take the Israelites into the Promised Land.

Remember the story of Rahab? It involves two spies, a scarlet cord, and redemption. Wow, God uses the most unsuspecting of persons to glorify Him, and Rahab is mentioned in the "Hall of Fame in Hebrews" and is in the hereditary line of Christ. Wow. Maybe He still has work for you and me!

"Thy word is a lamp unto my feet and a light unto my path."
Psalm 119:105

"Let no unwholesome word proceed from your mouth."
Ephesians 4:29

III.

One more quote:

"No matter how you feel, get up, dress up,
show up, and show up for life."
Regina Brett, Cleveland.com

IV. Prayer

Oh, Father, words are so powerful because *you are the word* and from you springs a fountain of "words" to empower, enrich, encourage, and influence those around us. Be "in our words," Lord, as we speak from anointed lips, Amen and Amen.

V. Questions

1. Describe the power of words in your life.

2. Whose words have influenced you?

3. What were the favorite words of your spouses?

4. What are some words by which you have chosen to live?

5. If you could hear Jesus utter any words audible to you, what would they/it be?

6. Are there words you wish you had *not* spoken to your spouse?

7. Did you have a chance to say goodbye? Do you want to share those words?

8. When is it the hardest for you to discipline your words?

9. Share a time your words freed someone, encouraged them, or changed their course.

10. Did you sense God's favor?

Know the Lord

Safe Strong Place (God)
Naomi

I.

Good morning, beautiful ladies that I love.

My dear friend Captain Charlie Plumb, who was a POW and in solitary confinement, writes:

> When I returned from the torture of nearly six years in North Vietnamese prison camps, I found new challenges. I was the first Ex-POW to return to the Kansas City area and was approached by several ladies whose husbands, my fellow fighter pilots, were listed as MIA (Missing in Action). They wanted me to give them hope that their husbands were actually alive. "Your family prayed for you and you came home, we've been praying for our pilot. Surely God will answer our prayers as He did those of your family and our guy will come home too."
>
> The unfortunate truth was, in the prison camps we made great efforts to positively identify every POW. We knew who would be coming home and who was probably killed in action. In addition, I had seen several fellow pilots shot down at sea or over dense jungle with no parachute sighted. They were listed as MIA but it was highly probable that they were never coming home. My heart was broken for these military spouses. I prayed for an answer.

I found myself trying to give these ladies optimism yet be honest with them. It was not easy. The answer was to give them hope and comfort in Christ and ask them to accept His will and His grace.

II.

Bible verse for today:

> *"Oh, that we might know the Lord!*
> *Let us press on to know Him.*
> *He will respond to us as surely as the arrival of dawn*
> *Or the coming of rains in early spring."*
> *Hosea 6:3*

Love that.

III.

Quotes for today:

> *"Happiness is one of the greatest gifts of expectation!"*
> *Naomi*

> *"Consecrate yourselves for tomorrow. The Lord*
> *will do amazing things among you."*
> *Joshua 3:5*

> *"When he arrived and saw the grace of God, he was*
> *glad and encouraged all of them to remain true to*
> *the Lord with a firm resolve of the heart."*
> *Acts 11:23*

IV. Prayer

Dear Father, give me the perseverance and strength to strive to know you better every day. Help me understand and comprehend your plan for me and to trust completely in you for everything. Amen.

VIII. Questions

1. Do you make resolutions? What were they, and have you kept them?

2. Have you thought of the difference between resolutions and aspirations?

Aspirations: Thinking about future possibilities . . . recognizing that hope and faith are intertwined. Confidence and courage are intertwined.

Resolutions: A firm decision to take action.

3. If time and money were not a factor, what would your life be like at the end of the following year?

4. What would be the most fulfilling thing that happened?

5. So . . . for this year . . . what do you have the courage, confidence, faith, and hope to aspire to?

6. What do you have to let go of?

7. What do you need to grab God's hand for?

Thresholds

Safe Strong Place (God)
Naomi

I.

Good morning, dear ones . . .

II.

Interesting Thought to Muse on: Thresholds

This move we are making . . . seems to be a big one. For some reason . . . the packing is exhausting . . . the "shedding" is so difficult, not knowing the future . . . is always a challenge . . .

It *feels* like a "*threshold*" . . . and I am peering into the next room, the next chapter, the next "home" . . . and leaving the comfort and "knowing" of this one.

Does this sound familiar???

For each of you . . . crossing "thresholds" . . . is *not* new . . . and I am so proud of all of you and how you are doing it! I am just proud to know you. My "threshold" seems so insignificant in light of yours . . . .

It is interesting . . . that children/people with some brain disorder . . . have difficulty crossing a threshold. They have to go back and do it repeatedly to "get it perfect" . . . which, of course, is impossible . . .

Crossing thresholds takes courage, a sense of trust in what is coming next and your support system, and faith in God to meet it with peace and joy.

III. Prayer

Father, sometimes we feel like we are on the edge of a cliff, a huge threshold. Other times our days are filled with one small threshold to cross over after the other. Knowing you are in our steps, when we trust in you, keeps us safe from crossing haphazardly, without judgment . . . thank you, thank you, Amen.

IV. Questions

1. At which threshold are you now standing?

2. What is preventing you from crossing that threshold?

3. Does that threshold seem like a boundary or a frontier?

A Quiz: Score yourself 1–10, with 10 being the best.

1. Forgiveness

2. Grieving

3. Serving

4. Walking in love

5. Managing your emotions

6. Speaking the truth in love

7. Comforting when necessary

8. Accepting "no answer"

9. Letting God be your vindicator

10. Choosing to cross the next threshold!

Reflections on Loss

Safe Strong Place (God)
Naomi

I.

Good morning, women that I love.

Reflections on loss . . .

1. Parents

2. Siblings or close relatives

3. Friends

4. Heroes/celebrities

5. How we handle these losses prepares us for the huge loss . . . our spouse, cancer, etc.

6. What is our *rock* . . . what do we stand on? God's grace, love, and sovereignty!

II. Prayer

Precious Father, the certainties of our life in you are that you will always be there with us. That you know the path before we step on it, that you prepare us with wisdom and your grace, and the power of *knowing you* are our *sovereign Lord* . . . thank you, thank you! Amen.

III. Questions

Best Friend or Worst Enemy?

1. Draw a line down the center of a piece of paper from top to bottom . . .

2. Put *Worst Enemy* on the left side, and *Best Friend* on the right side.

3. Reflect on these statements:

    a. As our own worst enemies, we create inner conflicts and make it more challenging to do the things we want or need to do.

    b. As our own best friends, we bring unique skills, gifts, and qualities to whatever we do.

4. On the left column, list how you are your own worst enemy, making it more challenging to do the things you want or need to do.

5. As your own best friend, how can you apply your giftedness to negate the "worst enemy" and accomplish the best for God's glory?

6. Examine both columns . . . how can your "best friend" help your "worst enemy"?

7. Share with the group your conclusions . . .

8. Healing Promise: All we need to do is bring our broken dreams, our hurts to Jesus . . . he is our great healer!

> *"Then great multitudes came to Him, having with the
> lame, blind, mute, maimed, and many others and they
> laid them down at Jesus' feet, and He healed them."*
> *Matthew 15:30*

What do you have that needs to be healed . . . today?

Draw Near to God

Safe Strong Place (God)
Naomi

I.

Good morning, dear ones!

> *"Draw nigh to God, and he will draw nigh to you."*
> *James 4:8*

Musing this morning . . . huge question . . . dear ones:

1. When do you draw near to God?

2. How do you draw near to God?

3. When does he draw near to you?

4. How does he draw near to you?

I would like you to be musing on this and share it next week with us.

II.

Quick review of today's study:

1. Joshua 3. Wow, those Israelites disobey. They need a judge (leader) to help and God to lead them to win the next

battle. They are sorry for their sins. They win peace for eighty years or so. (Probably till they forget and start living in the sin of worshiping other gods again.)

2. 4 Classic Steps:

   a. Rebellion (usually happens in good times . . . sound familiar?)

   b. Repression . . . hardship

   c. Repentance . . . sorry/sorry/sorry!

   d. Restoration (purification leads to restoration)

Societies do this . . . We do this.

IV. Prayer

Father, when we study the history of your people, your chosen people in the Old Testament, we are amazed at how often they disregard and disobey *you*. You are so patient with them . . . you warn them, and warn them before they are punished for their disobedience. And then, we look inside of ourselves, and see some of the same patterns. We bow our heads in shame, and yet we *know* we can claim the forgiveness that *you* made possible for *your* children through the blood of Christ on Calvary. Thank you, thank you . . . Amen.

V. Questions

1. Do you have a worship/devotional routine?

2. What do you do when you are not feeling very spiritual?

3. How do you get freshly aligned with Him?

4. What devotionals/books do you use?

5. Do you ever feel your prayers are not heard? What do you do?

6. Why causes you to feel dry spiritually?

7. What verses help you most?

8. Is there a person/s that you might talk to about this besides the Lord?

9. What would you recommend to a believer that came to you?

Questions?

All right, here goes. I'm old. That means that I've survived (so far), and a lot of people I've known and loved did not. I've lost friends, best friends, acquaintances, co-workers, grandparents, mom, relatives, teachers, mentors, students, neighbors, and a host of other folks. I have no children, and I can't imagine the pain it must be to lose a child. But here's my two cents.

I wish I could say you get used to people dying. I never did. I don't want to. It tears a hole through me whenever somebody I love dies, no matter the circumstances. But I don't want it to "not matter."

I don't want it to be something that just passes. My scars are a testament to the love and relationship I had for and with that person. And if the scar is deep, so was the love. So be it. Scars are a testament to life. Scars are a testament that I can love deeply and live deeply and be cut, or even gouged, and that I can heal and continue to live and love. And the scar tissue is stronger than the original flesh ever was. Scars are a testament to life. Scars are only ugly to people who can't see.

As for grief, you'll find it comes in waves. When the ship is first wrecked, you're drowning, with wreckage all around you. Everything floating around you reminds you of the beauty and magnificence of the ship that was no more. And all you can do is swim. You find some piece of the wreckage, and you hang on for a while. Maybe it's some physical thing. Maybe it's a happy memory or a photograph. Maybe it's a person who is also floating. For a while, all you can do is float. Stay alive.

In the beginning, the waves are 100 feet tall and crash over you without mercy. They come ten seconds apart and don't even give you time to catch your breath. All you can do is hang on and float. After a while, maybe weeks, maybe months, you'll find the waves are still 100 feet tall, but they come further apart. When they come, they still crash all over you and wipe you out. But in between, you can breathe, you can function. You never know what's going to trigger the grief. It might be a song, a picture, a street intersection, the smell of a cup of coffee. It can be just about anything . . . and the wave comes crashing. But in between waves, there is life.

Somewhere down the line, and it's different for everybody, you find that the waves are only 80 feet tall. Or 50 feet tall. And while they still come, they come further apart. You can see them coming. An anniversary, a birthday, or Christmas, or landing at O'Hare. You can see it coming, for the most part, and prepare yourself. And when it washes over you, you know that somehow you will, again, come out the other side. Soaking wet, sputtering, still hanging on to some tiny piece of the wreckage, but you'll come out.

Take it from an old guy. The waves never stop coming, and somehow you don't really want them to. But you learn that you'll survive them. And other waves will come. And you'll survive them too. If you're lucky, you'll have lots of scars from lots of loves. And lots of shipwrecks.

GSnow on Grief : garysully1986 - reddit

Moving Forward

Safe Strong Place (God)
Naomi

I.

Moving day for the Rhodes!

The moving vans are arriving . . . and we have a full day ahead, moving from Scottsdale back to Phoenix.

II.

Losses . . . remember we talked about how the "many losses of life" add up to help us with the seemingly insignificant losses that come our way?

This is a loss. We love where we live . . . we love the house we live in . . . but when we sold our last house, we decided to lease to "downsize" (which we hardly did).

We have been in this house for five and a half years . . . with fantastic Christian landlords, and they want their home back to redo and retire.

So, in the meantime, and in between time, our daughter Katherine and family moved from Louisville to be close to us . . . and now we are moving to be close to them. Seven houses away . . . is not the neighborhood or home we would choose. . . *but* . . . the neighbors we definitely *would/will* choose . . . it is God's best for us now!

That being said . . . with loss comes challenges . . . I do not have the physical strength for this big move and am hoping I continue to have the emotional/spiritual strength for this big move.

Good news . . . it has a guest suite . . . and you are welcome to come and visit!

So . . . this is the last event of almost "anything" in this lovely home . . . we are saying goodbye, today . . . and hello to what is next!

So . . . do you "dare to muse" and acknowledge the blessings from your most significant loss? Are there some? Something to talk to the Lord about, perhaps!

I often refer to the "Welcome Prayer Book" (*Welcoming Prayer, Consent On The Go*, Contemplative Outreach).

Today I read:

Embrace the moment as it is.

Letting go gets to the obstacles in the unconscious.

We consent to be transformed, which includes dismantling of our emotional programs for happiness and healing of our unconscious.

Let go and let God!

This produces *freedom in our spirit*!

> *"He is so rich in kindness and grace that He purchased our*
> *freedom with the blood of His Son and forgave our sins."*
> *Ephesians 1:7*

III. Prayer

Father, there are so many hindrances that Satan would love to tempt us with . . . to be secure, to know where you will live, what you will do, who you will marry, will you have children, who will they marry? Help us to rest, to be revived by *your plans* for our lives . . . they are good plans, they are for our good, and the ministry to others of *your* love and grace.

We find *your* real freedom in this resting . . . thank you, Amen.

IV. Questions

The hindrances that need to be let go of are:

Our desire for security

Our need for affection

Our need for control

1. Which of those is most difficult for you and why?

2. Another muse: What is the difference between sympathy and empathy?

3. When do you experience sympathy . . . examples?

4. When do you experience empathy . . . examples?

God's Heart of Compassion

Safe Strong Place (God)
Naomi

I.

Dear ones,

Lessons I learned this week: huge moves are not for people our age!

We took too much "stuff" . . . primarily books! Good news . . . we are in a neighborhood that allows garage sales, so our daughter will have one for us to sell all the stuff we should not have brought with us. Being seven houses away from our daughter is *sweet*!

They stop in with their two dogs, who now know where we live when they go out for a walk! They had us over for dinner with three of their college friends last night!

We have not named the house yet . . . but it is two blocks from one of our Phoenix mountains, so Grace Mountain has been suggested. The last house was 7 Palms Sanctuary.

Devotional thoughts:

> *"His divine power has given us everything we need*
> *for life and godliness (through our knowledge of Him)*
> *who called us by His own glory and goodness."*
> *2 Peter 1:3*

II.

"In faith we know the Holy Spirit transforms
us, inside and out, in God's time."
"The Welcome Prayer" by Father Thomas Keating

"My thoughts are not your thoughts, and
my ways are not your ways."
Isaiah 55:8

Look further at Isaiah 55:6–9, and you will see the mystery of divine providence and the surprise of God's compassionate heart.

First, He tells us what to do . . . seek Him, call on Him, return to Him.

Second, He tells us why God will have compassion and abundantly pardon us, sweeping us into His arms!

"God's heart of compassion confounds our intuitive predilections
about how he loves to respond to his people if they would
but dump in his lap the ruin and wreckage of their lives.
He isn't like you. Even the most intense of human love is
but the faintest echo of heaven's cascading abundance."
"Gentle and Lowly" by Dane Orland
(Kingsway.cc, accessed 8/12/2022)

III.

He is a restorer:

"For you shall go out in joy and be led forth in peace. The
mountains and the hills before you shall break forth into
singing, and the trees of the field shall clap their hands!
I will dwell in the high and holy place and also with him

> *who is contrite and lowly in spirit to revive the spirit of*
> *the lowly and to revive the heart of the contrite. "*
> *Isaiah 55:12–13*

Wow . . . finally, "the faithful love of the Lord never ends."

> *"His mercies never cease. Great is His faithfulness, His*
> *mercies begin fresh each morning. The Lord is good to those*
> *who depend on Him, to those who search for Him. "*
> *Lamentations 3:22–23, 25*

IV. Prayer

Father, help us to stop and remember we are "called" to be *your* children, and that your mercies *are* new every morning . . . new starting of new days for *your* glory. We love you; we long to be helped in eternity by *you*, dear Father, Amen and Amen.

V. Questions

1. What lessons have *you* learned from last week or last month?

2. Have you ever named a home you have lived in? Share.

3. Your thoughts and experience with 2 Peter 1:3.

4. Has there ever been a time when it was tough for you to forgive?

5. Could I forgive you? Share.

6. Anything you wish you had shared with this group that you haven't?

Christ Loved You Before All Worlds

Safe Strong Place (God)
Naomi

I.

Good morning . . . guess what?

I feel at home . . . in our new home. Come see us . . . past the

"Narnia Door" to the upstairs Rhode Retreat, it is ready for you! And . . . we can have devotions in "The Sanctuary," and look out at Grace Mountain!

Yes . . . we name everything!

Except for the house. We still do not have a definite name for the house, just that it is seven doors from Katherine and Ken and eight minutes from Curt and Beth, Kylin, Eric, Esme, Dathan, Liza, Leo, and Tegren. Kaylee, Carsten, Atlas, and Castor are moving there soon. (Did you get all of that?) Oh, and Hannah has an apartment ten minutes away, Broder is at GSU fifteen minutes away, and "the boys" (Sammy and Buddy . . . Boston Terriers) live seven houses away and visit us on their nightly walks with their parents, Ken and Kath!

Family over location! Yeah!

II.

Some thoughts from my devotions this week: Friendship! Sometimes even more important than family!

And . . . isn't it amazing that He tells us that we are also His friends in Scripture! (John 15:14–15)

Love that—*our* sins are many, but His mercies are more . . . new every morning . . . *great* is His faithfulness!

We can live "for the heart of Christ" or "from the heart of Christ" . . . hmmm . . . interesting . . . which am I doing . . . which am I being?

Here is a great Spurgeon quote (just muse on it as I slowly share it):

> *"Christ loved you before all worlds; long ere the day star*
> *flung his ray across the darkness, before the wing of angels*
> *had flapped the unnavigated ether, before aught of creation*
> *had struggled from the womb of nothingness, God, even*
> *our God, had set His heart upon all His children.*
> *Since that time, has He once swerved, has He once turned*
> *aside, once changed? No; ye who have tasted of His love*
> *and known His grace will bear me witness that He has*
> *been a certain friend in uncertain circumstances!*
> *You have oft left Him; has He ever left you?*
> *You have had many trials and troubles; has He ever deserted you?*
> *Has He ever turned away His heart and*
> *shut up His bowels of compassion?*
> *No, children of God, it is your solemn duty to say*
> *'No,' and bear witness to his faithfulness."*

Don't you love that . . . it is your "solemn duty to bear witness to His faithfulness!"

III.

Now . . . quick highlight on your last week and most significant challenge. Who wants to jump in first?

IV. Prayer

Oh God of all mercy, we have all done things in our lives that have defied your will for us. Thank you for your unfailing love even when we have failed you. Please know that you are my living hope and refuge and wash away my sins with the cleansing blood of your son, Jesus. Amen.

V. Questions

Think about the word *mercy*.

> *"But God being rich in mercy, because of His*
> *great love with which He loved us."*
> *Ephesians 2:4*

1. When have you felt you needed mercy?

2. When have you extended mercy?

3. How is mercy different than grace?

Circle of Friends

Safe Strong Place (God)
Naomi

I.

Good morning, dear ones!

II.

Friendship: One of my favorite subjects!

> *"Oh, the comfort, the inexpressible comfort of feeling safe*
> *with a person; having neither to weigh thoughts nor*
> *measure words, but to pour them all out, just as they are,*
> *chaff and grain together, knowing that a faithful hand*
> *will take and sift them, keep what is worth keeping, and*
> *then, with a breath of kindness, blow the rest away."*
> *George Eliot (Quotetab.com, accessed 8/12/2022)*
> *"I shall no longer call you servants but friends."*
> *John 15:15*

III.

You are not alone!

Know that there are others who have suffered yet survived!

We are here to help.

We are still standing.

We stand in a circle, with our arms around each other!

We are blessed . . . Safe Strong Place, women!

IV. Prayer

Oh, Lord, our Lord, *you* are our best friend! And in *you* we find the lovely qualities we look for in earthly friendships. Father, I do believe that we become like the people we spend time with. Help us to be wise and to choose godly people, rich in your loveliness to be our closest friends. Amen.

V. Questions

1. Share qualities you look for in a close friend.

2. Share one of your closest friends . . . and why.

3. Do you think of Jesus as being your friend? Why or why not?

4. What are you free to share with your closest friend . . . What are you not free to share . . . maybe that you could even share with us?

Vision

Safe Strong Place (God)
Naomi

I.

Good morning, dear ones.

Do you love music? I do . . . and I love Christian music.

I play the piano and the organ, sang in a high school choir and church choirs (before I lost a vocal cord from my stroke) and I love the theology of the hymns.

A friend of mine sent me a book their choir made as a gift to a retiring choir director with favorite hymns to be used as prayers, not sung.

I started to use it in my morning God time . . . and it is one of my favorites! Listen and pull out a few concepts . . . as I did!

Be thou my vision, O Lord of my heart;
naught be all else to me, save that thou art.
Thou my best thought, by day or by night,
waking or sleeping, thy presence my light.
Be thou my wisdom, be thou my true word;
I ever with thee, and thou with me, Lord.
Born of thy love, thy child may I be,
thou in me dwelling and I one with thee.
Be thou my buckler, my sword for the fight.

Be thou my dignity, thou my delight,
thou my soul's shelter, thou my high tow'r.
Raise thou me heav'nward, O Pow'r of my pow'r.
Riches I heed not, nor vain empty praise;
thou mine inheritance, now and always.
Thou and thou only, first in my heart,
Ruler of heaven, my treasure thou art.
"*True Light of heaven, when vict'ry is won
may I reach heaven's joys, O bright heav'n's Sun!
Heart of my heart, whatever befall,
still be my vision, O Ruler of all.
"Be Thou My Vision: Old Irish Hymn," by Dallan Forgail, trans-
lated by Mary Elizabeth Byrne, Versifier Ellen Hull, public domain

So precious . . . what did you hear?

And then . . . from "the Welcome Prayer":

> *"Repression is a defense mechanism that prevents the*
> *unconscious from coming to the conscious."*

Wow.

Hmm . . . there just may be some questions about all this for next
week!

II.

Prayer . . . I need prayer . . . and that makes me keenly aware that
you do also . . . so quickly, each of you share one prayer . . . maybe
you could record them and send them to us: That will be our
prayer for today.

III. Questions

1. What is one huge challenge, problem, or event in your life that you have repressed?

2. Is there an "elephant on the table" in your family?

3. Has one ever been brought to light? Has that been healthy?

4. What is the advantage of bringing the repressed to the conscious mind?

5. Thoughts on highlights from the "Be Thou My Vision" song.

Your Story

Safe Strong Place (God)
Naomi

I.

Good morning . . . precious friends!

We are just back, late last night, from the Gaither Family Praise Fest in Gatlinburg, Tennessee.

It was a fantastic time of praise, prayer, and rededication to all we stand for and believe.

It was a time to memorialize those who have sacrificed their lives for us.

It was a time to reevaluate purpose, passions, and family friendships.

I am full to overflowing . . . and exhausted!

II.

This is a time to reevaluate our life purpose, passions, and the life of Samuel. This is an incredible God-serving year. Samuel was a man of *impact*! May it be so for us!

Samuel was a shepherd. He was relationally a kind, caring leader . . . even our Lord is described as a shepherd.

Samuel was a steward . . . he was a man of great responsibility . . . he acted on behalf of his master . . . do I? Do you?

Samuel was a seer. He possessed vision and communicated it to others.

Samuel was a servant. He gave up his rights for the sake of the master and others.

Classic Samuel quote:

> *"You have done a foolish thing,' Samuel said. 'You have not kept the command the Lord your God gave you; if you had, he would have established your kingdom over Israel for all time.'"*
> *1 Samuel 13:13*

Heavy!

Does the Lord "replace" us in such situations?

III. Prayer

Father, we learn richly from the stories of the saints in scripture. We also learn from those who have lived disobedient lives, who have squandered their gifts, their lives. May we realize the gift of each new day, week, month, year. May we enrich our stories for your glory as we seek to live the story of your Son, Jesus Christ, more fully. Amen.

IV. Questions

"I long to hear the story of your life." (Shakespeare)

Read the story of Samuel . . . excellent . . . will share it as we open next week!

1. What is your story?

2. What is the title of your story?

3. Do you have more than one title?

4. If you had to sum up the "story of your life" in one word, what would that word be?

5. If you were to sum up the "story of your life" in one paragraph, what would it be?

6. What would your main emphasis be in telling us your story?

7. What would you be tempted to "leave out"?

Triggers

Safe Strong Place (God)
Naomi

I.

Good morning, dear ones,

We are in California at the beach for five days; it is so delightful!

Catch-up time:

Share one of the most memorable events of this week.

II.

Have you ever thought of sacrifice in life . . . and the rewards of sacrifice?

A couple of powerful scripture verses:

> *"Look, I am coming soon! My reward is with me, and I will give to each person according to what they have done."*
> *Revelation 22:12*

> *"Rejoice and be glad, for great is your reward in heaven."*
> *Matthew 5:12*

"If we consider the 'unblushing' promises of reward and the staggering nature of the rewards promised in the Gospels, it would seem that Our Lord finds our desires not too strong, but too weak. We are half-hearted creatures, fooling about with drink and sex and ambition when infinite joy is offered us, like an ignorant child who wants to go on making mud pies in a slum because he cannot imagine what is meant by the offer of a holiday at the sea."
C.S. Lewis

III. Prayer

Oh, Lord, as I sit on the shore of *your* mighty ocean, feeling the power of the waves, seeing the whales breaching in the sunshine, and the dolphins playing joyfully, I am thankful that I am not wasting my time "making mud pies on the shore"! Glory to your name, majestic is your power, dear Lord, Amen.

IV. Questions

We were honored that you shared with all who share in this safe place. Our hearts are so with you! We are praying for the group.

Let's talk about *triggers*!

1. What is your experience on the anniversary day of your husband's journey to Jesus?

2. What plans/strategies have you used that have made this an easier time?

3. How often do you reflect on the blessings of your marriage versus the sadness of the loss of your best friend?

4. Share how you approach deep sadness . . . do you go inward and "hide," or do you choose to share it with someone close who cares?

5. What works best for you?

6. Are holidays big triggers or diversions?

7. Do you have words of scripture or songs that are most helpful to comfort?

8. Is there a place you go to be by yourself and grieve, remember, and celebrate the joys of your journey with your husband?

Remembering

Safe Strong Place (God)
Naomi

I.

Good morning . . . it is *hot* here! OK . . . complaining after that great week at the beach! But still great to be home.

II.

Father's Day on Sunday:

My dad was Virgil Asbury Reed. He had a master's in education, was a school superintendent, then a Boy Scout executive for years.

He was an amazing man of God.

During WWII, he was ordained as a pastor to fill the place of pastors that went to war to be chaplains.

I sat in the front row of those small Minnesota towns and was spellbound by his sermons . . . my father's hand.

He died on Good Friday (I was thirteen). He was so godly; I thought he would rise from the dead.

Sunday morning, he was not there . . . but I *knew* he had not died!

Daddies that love Jesus never die; they just close their eyes and go to His house to wait for us!

III.

Share something about your dad.

IV.

Word and definition for the day:

Palingenesis: means rebirth or recreation. In the Bible, palingenesis is described by Jesus in John 3 when He tells Nicodemus that only those who are born again can see heaven. Peter refers to the idea in 1 Peter 1:3: "Blessed be the God and Father of our Lord Jesus Christ! According to his great mercy, he has caused us to be born again to a living hope through the resurrection of Jesus Christ from the dead." Also, see 1 Peter 1:23, Titus 3:5, 1 Corinthians 6:11, and Revelation 7:14 for references to regeneration and renewal.

V.

In the finale of the book *Les Miserables* by Victor Hugo, Jean Valjean sacrificed a lot! He was misunderstood, maligned, hunted, forgotten, and then . . . at the end of his life, his story was told rightly!

"But we see his great heart, his sacrificial choices, and at the end, we see he is finally vindicated . . . how he did the most loving and sacrificial thing, how his life was filled with beauty and dignity. And . . . then . . . the great cloud of witnesses shows up for his arrival into the kingdom of heaven, and he deserves it."

I went to a funeral yesterday of a good friend, Dr. Ion Lamont. He was our kids' orthodontist and had been to many of our seminars.

He was on the one in Greece with Beth and Tom. He was gentle, kind, and honorable.

They had three sweet kids. They grew up with ours. One was killed in a drug-related incident. There was so much sadness in his life.

How do you begin to tell the story of a human life? How can you do justice to all the hidden sorrow, the valiant fight, the millions of tiny, unseen choices, and the impact of a great soul on thousands of lives? Only in the Kingdom of God will we know . . . will others know the real story of his life, of your husband's life, of your life.

And . . . his ashes were there in a little box . . .

But he wasn't . . . he was and is with Jesus!

VI. Prayer

Father, I will never forget walking through the house looking for my earthly father . . . only to realize that he had *not* died; he had gone to live with you, his Heavenly Father. Thank you for the assurance you gave me of my relationship eternally to you as a twelve-year-old girl, dear Lord. May we bask in the knowledge that you are our Father, and always with us . . . always, amen and amen.

VII. QUESTIONS

1. Share feelings about "remembering" . . . or did you choose to ignore and forget; if so, why?

2. Was there something you loved doing with your spouse in the summertime? Vacation time?

3. How could you do some of that again with your kids or friends?

4. Have you experienced deep or moderately deep depression?

5. What was your solution?

6. Have you dealt closely with others with deep depression?

7. Do people who die from suicide go to heaven?

Tragedies

Safe Strong Place (God)
Naomi

I.

Good morning, dear ones!

Let's start with an exciting verse from 2 Corinthians 6:10: *"sorrowful, yet always rejoicing."* That jumped out at me . . . does that ever happen to you?

Wow!

1. Paul talks about rejoicing in both situations . . . because they so often run consecutively!

2. Good things and bad things are always happening, all the time in our lives . . . this is "normal Christian living."

3. We should not always think of them as calamities . . . though calamities happen worldwide every minute!

And . . . this follows:

> *"Develop an attitude of gratitude. Say thank you to*
> *everyone you meet for everything they do for you."*
> *Brian Tracy (blog.gratefullness.me, accessed 8/12/2022)*

II.

What are your thoughts on why:

1. Unbelieving people often wake up through pain and loss? I was coaching a woman through hard times and asked her where she was "spiritually" . . . she said, "Oh my god, I don't believe there is a god."

2. True tragedies are true calamities . . . that we pray for and care deeply about? Read the book *The Choice*. We get involved in these as believers. We support these monetarily and through prayer. They stretch our realities. We are not the only hurting ones.

Historically there have been many tragedies: six million Jews were killed, sixty million Russians starved and killed in the gulags, 1.5 million Armenians were slaughtered in 1915, and a million Rwandans were killed in 1994.

Some calamities are pure evil . . .

Losses of loved ones are personal tragedies that are real, close, not distant. Why? Hmmmmm . . . God's sovereignty!

Our spiritual growth continues as we learn to trust in Him for our loneliness, our lack of wisdom in decision-making . . . etc. A meandering of thoughts summed up in the hymn "How Sweet The Name of Jesus" by John Newton.

Pray it with me . . . as I sum up what it says:

How sweet the name of Jesus sounds
in a believer's ear!
It soothes our sorrows, heals our wounds,
and drives away our fear.
It makes the wounded spirit whole
and calms the troubled breast;
'tis manna to the hungry soul,
and to the weary, rest.

O Jesus, shepherd, guardian, friend,
my Prophet, Priest, and King,
my Lord, my Life, my Way, my End,
accept the praise I bring.
How weak the effort of my heart,
how cold my warmest thought;
but when I see you as you are,
I'll praise you as I ought.
Till then I would your love proclaim
with every fleeting breath;
and may the music of your name
refresh my soul in death.
"How Sweet the Name of Jesus Sounds." Psalter Hymnal, 1987.
John Newton/Lloyd Larson (Hymnary.com, accessed 8/12/2022)

Accept the praise I bring . . . Amen and amen.

III. Prayer

Oh, Father, there is a blanket of sadness and buckets of tragedy in our lives and the lives of those we love. We try in our own strength to "make sense" of these tragedies, only to come to dead ends in our faith at times. And then, if we listen, you are *always* there for us, to comfort, to guide, to clear our minds and hearts for the gratitude and goodness of life also. What would we do without you? We love you, Lord. Amen.

IV. Questions

I started out today by mentioning gratitude: Gratitude is a requirement for happiness and goodness!

Hmmm . . . Most people remember the bad done to them for longer than the good done to them.

1. On a scale of 1–10, how would you rate yourself as a "grateful person"?

2. Is there a blazing example of remembering the bad instead of the good in your life?

3. a. With your spouse?

4. b. With someone else?

5. Have you dealt with that? Forgiven that? Forgotten that, or does it spring up often? Why do you think that happens? What do you do with it?

6. Are there scriptures that "spring up for you" when the bad is remembered instead of the good? Is there any merit in that?

7. Who usually wins?

Final thoughts

Victor Frankl said, "*After security, man's greatest need is for meaning.*"

Let's think about that for next week!

Blessings, Naomi

Lids

Safe Strong Place (God)
Naomi

I.

Good morning!

I just came home from the National Speakers Association. I spoke at the Interdenominational Christian Worship Service (which we started in the early '80s.). It was so special: Salt and Light Groups and the challenge to share our faith in the secular world. The call on my life . . . and all of our lives is to "go and tell/teach the gospel . . . the good news"!

II.

Another hymn:

> *Guide me, O my great Redeemer,*
> *pilgrim through this barren land;*
> *I am weak, but you are mighty;*
> *hold me with your powerful hand.*
> *Bread of heaven, bread of heaven,*
> *feed me now and evermore,*
> *feed me now and evermore.*

Open now the crystal fountain,
where the healing waters flow.
Let the fire and cloudy pillar
lead me all my journey through.
Strong Deliverer, strong Deliverer,
ever be my strength and shield,
ever be my strength and shield.

When I tread the verge of Jordan,
bid my anxious fears subside.
Death of death, and hell's Destruction,
land me safe on Canaan's side.
Songs of praises, songs of praises
I will ever sing to you,
I will ever sing to you.

"Guide Me, O Thou Great Jehovah" by William Williams,
translated by Peter Williams. Psalter Hymnal. (Hymnary.org,
8/12/2022)

III.

I came across an interesting concept in the *Maxwell Leadership Bible Commentaries*. It is called "The Law of the Lid: leadership ability determines a person's level of effectiveness. It seems simple but is quite complex."

We are leaders in God's Kingdom . . . we are given people to "example." We are given people to teach to lead, whether children, grandchildren, great-grands, friends, neighbors, Bible studies . . . or complex professional challenges!

The more significant the impact you want to make, the greater your influence needs to be!

I have been studying Saul and David . . . wow, what a contrast!

David lifted lids . . . Saul kept the lids clamped down:

Both received counsel from godly men.

Both faced great challenges.

Both had the choice to change and grow.

Lids did not limit David; he had many internal and external lids.

1. His family (he was the youngest . . . least likely to be chosen)

2. His leader (Saul)

3. His background (poor shepherd family)

4. His youthfulness and inexperience.

Ultimately: David became a great leader, not because he lacked limitations in his life . . . but in spite of them.

Abide with me: fast falls the eventide;
the darkness deepens; Lord, with me abide.
When other helpers fail and comforts flee,
Help of the helpless, O abide with me.

Swift to its close ebbs out life's little day;
earth's joys grow dim, its glories pass away.
Change and decay in all around I see.
O thou who changest not, abide with me.

I need thy presence every passing hour.
What but thy grace can foil the tempter's power?
Who like thyself my guide and strength can be?
Through cloud and sunshine, O abide with me.

I fear no foe with thee at hand to bless,
ills have no weight, and tears no bitterness.
Where is death's sting? Where, grave, thy victory?
I triumph still, if thou abide with me.
Hold thou thy cross before my closing eyes.
Shine through the gloom and point me to the skies.

Heaven's morning breaks and earth's vain shadows flee; in life, in death, O Lord, abide with me.

"Abide with Me" by Henry Francis Lyte (Henry Francis Lyte, Hymnary.org accessed 8/12/2022)

IV. Prayer

Your abiding presence, Lord, is our comfort, our guide, our continuity amidst the disturbances of daily life. Your abiding presence is with us when we sit by the dying, the bereaved, and grieving ourselves. You hold us, you heal us, you help us. Thank you for your eternal presence in our lives, Amen.

V. Questions

1. What were "lids" that you had growing up?

2. Did you bring any of those lids into your marriage?

3. What lids have you had and "raised" in your marriage?

4. How do "lids" affect you without your husband . . . versus when he was with you?

5. Do you have a "lid" on your dialogue in our group?

6. What is it, and why do you not raise that "lid"?

7. What (outside of your marriage) has been an excellent lid riser for you? (NSA President for me!)

8. Ultimately, where do we get the power to break through heavy "lids"?

Covid Free. Praise God.

Safe Strong Place (God)
Naomi

I.

Naomi is COVID negative . . . Praising god. (After a harrowing close call and hospitalization for COVID.)

Thank you, dear Kathy, for all you have done for us and me during this COVID journey.

II.

This is a holy day . . . a holy moment . . . when I get to reflect on seeing you all on the call this morning . . . after my hospital ordeal . . . And that it was! I felt I would not come out alive . . . and I *know* your prayers carried me through that time.

I just had "no fight" in me . . . just soooooooooo sick. Now I humbly ask you to continue to pray for strength (I have almost none), rest, renewal . . . and learning to listen more than talk to the Lord!

III.

Reflections on my devotions today: It is intriguing how often the "word," the "concept" of "place" continues to arise for me. And, that we named this Safe Strong Place (God) . . . before I thought so much about that word. And the joy of knowing that God is always in that/this place.

I am just finishing *A Burning in My Bones: the Biography of Eugene Peterson*. Wow, he was such an exciting servant/saint, conflicted often, a person with God's hand firmly guiding the writing of *The Message*.

He is now in the last part of his life (as am I). He and his precious wife have left Regent University (where he was a professor for five years) and moved back to their Montana lake home . . . to rest, retire, and entertain. They have two guest rooms, and 152 guests in one year!

Eugene Peterson says: "He relished this quotidian life, a spirituality fully embedded in the particulars of their place."

> *"Ascribe to the Lord . . . glory and strength . . . The splendor*
> *of holinesss . . . The powerful voice of the Lord."*
> *Psalm 29*

> *The Lord is my rock*
> *The Lord is my refuge*
> *The Lord is my shield*
> *The Lord is the horn of my salvation*
> *The Lord is worthy of praise!*
> *"The wave of death swirled around me, in my distress, I called*
> *to the Lord, and He heard my cry. He reached down from on*
> *high and took hold of me. He drew me out of deep waters and*
> *was my support. He brought me out into a spacious place."*
> *2 Samuel 22:5*

You, Lord, are my lamp; you turn the darkness into light!

IV. Prayer

May we bless you when we can hardly breathe, Lord, in hospitals sterile. May we bless you when our bodies are recovering and breathing is easier again. May we bless you when the doorbell rings and friends bring a hot meal to bless us. May we bless you when we realize we have been given renewed life to live for you and your calling for our lives. Amen.

V. Questions.

1. What is the meaning of "quotidian life" for you?

2. What is the spirituality that is fully embedded in the particulars of the 'place' you are in? (How is God meeting you *now?*)

3. I am also fascinated by the concept these days of "seasons of our lives." What would you name this season . . . of your life?

4. David talks about the Lord bringing him out into a "spacious place" . . . Is your current space a spacious one? Share how that is in reality for you.

> *Amazing Grace, how sweet the sound*
> *That saved a wretch like me!*
> *I once was lost, but now am found,*
> *Was blind, but now I see.*
> *The Lord has promised good to me,*
> *His word my hope secures;*
> *He will my shield and portion be*
> *As long as life endures!*
> *"Amazing Grace" by E. O. Excell and John Newton*

Just As We Are

Safe Strong Place (God)
Naomi

I.

Good morning, dear ones.

II.

Today, we start with a prayer and a well-known hymn made famous by a well-known evangelist (you probably have already guessed it).

Pray it with me: Father, we come to you just as we are!

> *We come without a single plea, but that*
> *your blood was shed for me.*
> *Lamb of God. . . I come, we come.*
> *Just as I am and waiting not, to rid my soul of one*
> *dark blot . . . not a single one. Because your blood*
> *can cleanse each spot . . . I come, I come.*
> *Just as I am. . . tossed about with conflicts and doubts, fightings*
> *and fears, within, without . . . O Lamb of God, I come!*
> *Just as we are . . . poor, wretched, blind,*
> *all in Thee I find . . . I come.*

Just as I am . . . you will receive, will welcome, pardon, cleanse, relieve . . . because Thy promise I believe, I come, I come.
"Just as I Am" by Charlotte Elliott

III.

Come rest in Him.

1. I love an invitation . . . do you? What was a fantastic invitation you had once? In eighth grade, I was the head of the magazine drive for the school, and I worked in the office for a few weeks . . . out of class. Wow!

2. "The Lord then said to Noah, 'Go into the ark, you and your whole family, because I have found you righteous in this generation.'" Genesis 7:1

3. The first invitation was to Noah and his family to enter the ark, leaving everything behind . . . which took a lot of faith!

4. One of the first invitations the Lord gives us is to "come and find rest in Him" . . . leave everything behind. He is our "safe ark" . . . when the waters rise and the thunder roars.

5. Jesus, by faith, went to the cross. He accepted God's invitation to die for *our* sins . . . astonishing.

6. Are you hearing any invitation specifically right now from Him?

IV.

Quotes:

"All our feelings are gifts and teachers,
not enemies we need to avoid!"
The Welcome Prayer

Receptive Prayer

The life of Christ was a life of continuous receptive prayer:

> *"I can do nothing on my own authority. I seek not my*
> *will but the will of Him Who sent Me."* John 5:30

V. Prayer

Father, when this song is sung, I think of the thousands of people who "came to you" through the Billy Graham crusades, when that song was sung. The power of words . . . and your word . . . "come" . . . just as you are! We are pretty ragged, rough-edged people, Lord, and *you* accept us just as we are and then transform us! Holy, holy, holy . . . art thou, Amen.

IV. Questions

1. What feeling have you had that you can see now is a gift or a teacher? Is this a change? If so, how did that happen?

2. Do you believe Jesus was indeed in constant prayer, receiving and responding to the Father? Where is one place you picture Jesus praying? Is there a place you love to pray?

3. Is there an area in your life that God shows you needs to be refined? What is it?

4. Is there something you need to "lay at His feet for forgiveness" that you have not yet? Why? Does it feel good to "hang on to it"?

The Big Invitation

Safe Strong Place (God)
Naomi

I.

Good morning from beautiful Sedona.

It is so special to be here for five days. We are thrilled to be in this place we love with the red mountains, the blue skies, great restaurants, and time to just "be," with very few "have to's"!

II.

Ed Hackney called me the other day with a couple of Bible verses for you.

I do not remember seeing these verses . . . they will give you lots to muse on . . . if you let them!

> *"The righteous perish,*
> *and no one takes it to heart;*
> *the devout are taken away,*
> *and no one understands*
> *that the righteous are taken away*
> *to be spared from evil.*
> *Those who walk uprightly*

enter into peace;
they find rest as they lie in death. "
Isaiah 57:1–2

Raise your hand if you remember ever reading those verses?

Any thoughts?

III.

Last week, I focused on "a word" . . . the word *invitation!*

We also prayed the hymn "Just As I Am" . . . which was used at the end of every one of Billy Graham's evangelical messages, as the invitation to come forward if you were interested in responding to God's call for salvation.

That certainly is *the big invitation.*

There are so many others:

1. Wedding invitations

2. Graduation invitations

3. Housewarming invitations (do they still do that?)

4. Join our Bible study or our small group invitations

5. Will you be my friend invitations

6. Be a business partner

7. Come to our university and or professional program

Last week, I mentioned several Bible invitations . . . Noah to the ark, and ultimately we are invited into "the ark" of God's family and eternity with Him.

IV. Prayer

Lord, you sometimes "take us" to remove us from the evil that would prevail in and on our lives. May we trust in your plan for our loved ones and for ourselves. Amen.

V. Questions

1. Make a list of important invitations in your life.

2. Circle the ones that are very precious and changed your life (versus more casual invitations)

3. Have you ever been extended a negative invitation? Did you accept it? What were the consequences? Did you reject it, and if so, what were the consequences?

4. What was a totally unexpected invitation you were given?

5. Would you rather invite people to your home or be invited to theirs, and why?

6. Is there an invitation in your life that you consider extremely "holy" totally of God? How did that invitation change your life?

7. Are invitations gifts, or can they also be obligations?

Evil in the World

Safe Strong Place (God)
Naomi

I.

Good morning . . . It *is* a good morning! We fly today to Santa Barbara for our grandson Titus Rhode and Jess' wedding.

Many prayers asked for . . . for a peaceful/joyful wedding . . . without the trauma of an unhappy family member. And . . . we need prayer that I will have enough oxygen on the plane!

II.

Thoughts about the last week:

For some reason, the world situation piled up on me this weekend.

Then, all the 9-11 reviews were shown. It was so tragic . . . remembering . . . anyone want to share where you were or your thoughts this weekend? Did it all pile up on your soul also? Is it hard to comprehend the evil, the terrible evil, in this world? *How long, oh Lord, how long?*

III. Prayer

Father, we find ourselves so needed. We have a need for *your* oxygen to fill our lungs of faith in difficult situations. Your presence is what we need for wading through the mire of relationships that are difficult. Thank you for always being with us! Amen.

IV. Questions

1. How do you think the grief you experience over the loss of your spouse helps you comfort others . . . example?

2. What in our world situation grieves you most deeply? Is there anything you can personally do about it?

3. How much of your grief and handling of grief/sadness do you share with your children or grandchildren . . . why or why not? Example?

4. When you are sad about your loss or the huge losses in our world, what spiritual help do you go to . . . verses of scripture or prayer?

Keep All That Is Helpful Good and Useful

Safe Strong Place (God)
Naomi

I.

Good morning women that I love!

Beginning thoughts: After last week's session on the state of the evil in the world and how that affects us, let's focus on the good things!

Remember all that has blessed you!

Remember what you have learned!

Remember what your heart has felt!

Remember what your body has experienced!

Keep all that is helpful, good, and useful.

(Perhaps go around the circle with quick answers.)

Now:

I look forward to the day ahead . . .

I look forward to your life . . .

Know that you will be lighter, stronger, more accessible, more able to love . . .

Think of all those you will meet in your life . . .

Think of all you want to do in your life!

How are all these things different *now* . . . with today's perspective?

> *"THE HEALING TIME!*
> *Finally, on my way to 'yes.'*
> *I bump into all the places where I said 'no.'*
> *In my life*
> *All the untended wounds*
> *The red and purple scars*
> *Carved into my skin, my bones,*
> *Those coded messages*
> *That sends me down*
> *The wrong street again and again*
> *Where I find them*
> *The old wounds*
> *The old misdirections*
> *And I lift them*
> *One by bone*
> *Close to my heart*
> *And I say holy, holy, amen."*
> *"The Welcoming Prayer" by Father Thomas*
> *Keating, Contemplative Outreach*

What does this make you think of?

And this to muse on:

> *"You seek perfection*
> *And you meet all that happens to you.*
> *All you suffer, all you do, all your inclinations*
> *Are mysteries under which God gives Himself to you*
> *While you are vainly straining after high-flown fancies."*
> *Jean-Pierre Caussade in Abandonment to Divine Providence*

And then . . . God's promise amidst it all:

> *"Even to your old age and gray hairs, I am He, I*
> *am He who will sustain you, and I will carry you; I*
> *have made you, I will sustain and rescue you!"*
> *Isaiah 16:4*

II. Prayer

You promise to sustain us, to rescue us . . . and you also promise to love us, to hold us, to comfort us, and to fill empty places, empty spaces. Thank you, Lord. Amen.

III. Questions

1. What do you want to do in your life?

2. What do you look forward to in the future?

3. What are your greatest blessings?

The Chapel of My Heart Is Prayer

Safe, Strong Place (God)
Naomi

I.

Good morning! It is getting a tad, just a bit cooler in Arizona!

We are just home from an amazing three days in High Point, North Carolina, for the celebration of the opening of a massive conference center, hotel, restaurant, arena, children's museum . . . all built by our dear friend, the President of High Point, Nido Qubein. There were one thousand for a sit-down dinner the first night, five thousand for a concert the second night, one thousand for worship service with John Maxwell speaking and Lee Greenwood and Willie Jollie singing. It was a fantastic time. *All* was paid for *everyone* by Nido. He paid for dinner for all five thousand people, and he came to America from Lebanon to be a student himself at High Point with $30. He could not speak English.

But . . . he knows Jesus . . . and the power of His empowerment and prayer!

II.

Verse for today:

> *"All scripture is inspired by God. All His promises. All*
> *His commands for abundant living in Him!"*
> 2 *Timothy 3:16*

III.

I have been practicing receptive prayer . . . first on my patio . . .
and this morning, He said to me . . . "Be calm and be grateful."

IV.

Title for today: The Chapel of My Heart Is Prayer!

> *"What sweet relief we find in utter dependence on God."*
> *"Welcoming Prayer," Contemplative Outreach*

Why pray?

1. It is like talking to your best friend (God).

2. For God to change me.

3. He also changes our circumstances.

4. A prayer journal helps.

5. Prayer invites us into dependence.

6. We throw off our delusions of self-reliance and acknowl-edge that God *is* God . . . and we are not!

7. Prayer is a life-giving invitation rather than a guilt-ridden "should" on our spiritual to-do list.

"Welcoming Prayer," Contemplative Outreach

Text: 2 Kings 20

Hezekiah is dying; Isaiah is called in and affirms this, "Put your house in order."

Hezekiah wept bitterly, "Oh, Lord, remember me; I have walked faithfully."

Isaiah, while walking in the courtyard, heard God say, "Go back and tell Hezekiah that I have heard his prayer, and will heal him, and give him fifteen more years" . . . and He did.

God answers prayer!

V. Prayer

Father, we so often have our prayers answered in surprising ways, and we forget it is your wisdom that constructs the answers and not our own. Thank you, in thee do we trust, Amen.

VI.

Last week's questions

Love the book we are reading on interruptions!

VII. Questions

1. We talked about prayer . . . share the pluses and minuses of your prayer life.

2. Have you ever felt you had a real miracle answer to prayer as Hezekiah had (healed and given fifteen more years to life)? Share.

3. Is there someone in your life whose prayers deeply touch "the chapel of your heart"?

4. Do you pray with grown children . . . why or why not?

5. Who is your closest "prayer buddy" . . . the person you call when you need prayer?

What Do We Hang On To?

Safe, Strong Place (God)
Naomi

I.

November 8, 2021

Good morning, precious ones.

We are in the midst of a twenty-one-day trip. We went first to Minnesota to be at the celebration of our best man and dear friend, Don Watkins, who received a very prestigious award for service to the Scouts and Rotary.

Then to "the Ark." This is a museum rebuilding of Noah's ark. Noah invited them to come in . . . and they did . . . .to safety . . . to salvation from "the flood." Just as Christ is our ark, and invites us to come into safety, to salvation!

Then we spent three days of morning and evening concerts with the Collingsworth Family Singers, and speakers par excellent. I shared some of this with you last week.

Following a wonderful dinner in Louisville last night with our grandson, Dr. Haaken Reed Magnuson (yes, we are proud of him). This morning, we will surprise our precious friend, Liz Curtis Higgs, with flowers before she speaks to her Bible study at her church in Louisville. Tomorrow, we take a flight to Florida . . . and board the ship on Thursday.

This morn, reading the end of a book on "interruptions," I came to a page on "letting go"! Powerful!

There is a sweet story of the author's son, who loved to collect acorns. He found one and put it in a jar. Later he wanted to get it out to take it to his collection. This little boy put his hand in the jar and could not get his hand out. So he carried the jar around the yard, refusing to let go of the acorn . . . thus not releasing his hand! It made me wonder what we hang on to.

(Questions below will reflect on this thought.) Just a quick "muse" . . . Jonah ended up in a whale because he could not give up his "own way" for God's way!

II. Prayer

Father, what is it that you want me to "let go of"? May I listen "loudly" to the answer, may I release my fist that holds tightly to "stuff," to relationships, to priorities, and release to your loving plan for my life! I need your power to release . . . help me, Lord! Amen.

III. Questions

1. Is there anything (a mindset, a relationship, an ambition, a lifestyle) you would not relinquish if He asked you to do so . . . how would you know that He did?

2. Could He ask something of you that you would simply not do?

3. Has this ever happened? What did you do?

4. Did you ever go to Tarshish instead of Nineveh?

5. How did that turn out for you?

6. Where are you now . . . in Tarshish, Nineveh, or the belly of the whale?

7. What is next . . . what is God asking of you?

Yes . . . this is a rather heavy spiritual group of questions . . . but it is the finale of the book of interruptions . . . We fight the spiritual battle instead of letting Him win them for us.

Interruptions

Safe Strong Place (God)
Naomi

I.

Good morning! It is lovely to be back home and with you.

I have posted the book *Life Interrupted* by Pricilla Shirer. Thank you, Luan.

Priscilla is a great author. I love her analogies of Noah's journey in and out of God's will with our life journey.

In chapter 4, she writes about: *second chances.*

It is powerful to realize all the second chances God provides in the midst of our disobedience . . . when there is true repentance.

I love the examples:

Paul: "I am chief among sinners"

Peter: Made multiple promises to God that he did not keep

Jonah: Turned and ran in the opposite direction

God: Seeks and salvages those He loves

God: In compassion offers a second chance, and does that for us also

III. Rinse and repeat. Time to refocus on "not just to go" this is our "call" . . . to "be going" in obedience. Each day of our lives.

II. Prayer

Oh, Lord, Jonah's story is so "human," and you are so divine. Show me when I have gone my way and missed your best plan for my life. And, thank you when you have blessed me with wisdom beyond my years many times in choices I have made. Thank you, thank you, Amen.

III. Questions

1. Do you remember a time when you went in the opposite direction from the perfect will of God?

2. What was the "whale" that swallowed you?

3. What was it like to be the opposite of His will?

4. Did you get a second chance?

5. What is the first thing you think of as a "second chance" in your life?

6. Do you feel you are in a period of "second chance" now? What is it?

7. The bottom line is *obedience.* What are your thoughts?

8. Do you think there may be a "second chance" waiting for you? What would it be? How would your family handle this second chance for you?

Be Wise and Be Kind

Safe Strong Place (God)
Naomi

I.

Dear ones, last year, my phrase was: *trust and be a light bearer.* My new phrase is now: *wise words with kindness.*

> *"When she speaks, her words are wise, and*
> *she gives instructions with kindness."*
> *Proverbs 31:26*

May it be so.

What is your word for this year. . . And review last year's word!

II.

Challenge: Write a list of all your blessings in the last year and put them in your journal.

Write a list of the hard times, also.

My blessing outweighs my hardships . . . including almost dying and having significant identity theft!

How could you even begin to equate that with the miracle of the birth of great-grandchildren Tegrin, Esme, and Ragnar, and weddings of Wynston and Chyna, Titus and Jess, and recovery from COVID and help from grandson with identity theft?

God provides.

III.

Our pastor, Jamie Rasmussen, wrote a new book this year . . . One of my favorite chapters is "Way 5, Creating God Room in Your Life."

The opening story of Franklin Graham's return to the Lord is especially dear! His spiritual mentor was Bob Pearce, who started World Vision, which our son, Mark, was VP of for many years.

When my mother died, we found in her records that she had sent $1.00 per month to Bob Pearce for years and years. It was so dear!

We need to give God room to work in our lives. Sometimes after we have done all we can to meet a goal we believe God wants us to meet, we have to stop and pray and give God the room to work things out.

And . . . you wait:

1. Patiently

2. Expectantly

3. Actively

4. Joyfully

> *"Behold, this is our God for whom we have waited that He might save us. This is the Lord for whom we have waited: Let us rejoice and be glad in his salvation."*
> *Isaiah 25:9 NASB*

BE WISE AND BE KIND

IV. Prayer

Father, we are all "waiting" for something! And we are *all* waiting for *your* second coming. Bless our patience, may we share that blessing with others . . . Amen.

III. Questions

1. Have you ever "thought" or experienced the "God Room" concept?

2. When you look back on 2021, is there a time when you believe that God answered and "filled the gap"?

3. Is there something in your life now . . . that you are facing and needing completion, answers, solutions, and guidance for that needs God to "fill the gap"?

Worthy Pursuits

Safe Strong Place (God)
Naomi

I.

Good morning . . . great new week . . . to serve the Lord and be glad in Him, His holiness, His sovereignty, His plans for our lives . . . How wondrous, beyond understanding!

II.

His pursuits!

Hmmm . . . fun word . . . *pursuits*!

Webster says:

the act of pursuing: in pursuit of the fox; an effort to secure or attain; quest: the pursuit of happiness; any occupation, pastime, or the like, in which a person is engaged regularly or customarily; literary dreams.

III.

This week, I pursued:

1. Bible study in Ecclesiastes and Psalm 3

2. Visit with friends from high school, a Christian high school in Minneapolis . . . sweet afternoon of delight with Beth K., Kathy D., and four of Beth's key gals, including her daughter . . . there were questions of course . . . so special!

3. More "streaks" in my hair!

4. And . . . a shingles shot. . . and some aftereffects!

5. Bible studies and church, dinners with friends . . . coaching, and office work.

IV.

Time to "muse":

1. Is this consistent with my priorities?

2. Can someone else do it better?

3. Is this within my area of competence?

4. What do my trusted friends say?

5. Do I have the time?

V.

Quotes

"King Solomon pursued several unrelated goals
in a vain attempt to satisfy himself."
Ecclesiastes 2:1–11

He reached great success and felt unfulfilled and empty. Miserable, in fact!

He did not identify what he *really* wanted! Wow.

VI.

Prayer

Oh . . . we need your guidance, Lord. The world has priorities for us, ladders of success to climb, people to impress, places to go for meaning. And, your word says to us, that *you* are the only real source of fulfillment. *You* are more than enough, and that this light should shine in and through us to a dark world that knows nothing of true contentment. May it be so! Amen.

VI. Questions

1. What did you pursue and accomplish this week?

2. What did you pursue and *not* accomplish this week?

3. What do you wish you had pursued this week?

4. What would you like to pursue this year?

5. What do you consider to be worthy work? Worthy pursuits?

Holiday Section

Kim Harms

Holidays and anniversaries are frequently difficult times for those who have lost their spouse. Those around you may recognize those difficulties for the major holidays like Christmas, Thanksgiving, and Easter, but oftentimes anniversaries such as your husband's birthday, death day, the date of your first meeting, or other days important to you as a couple may find you plummeting back down into the depths of the grief pit.

My husband, Jim, and I were veterans and we loved going out to dinner on Veteran's Day to a restaurant that offered free meals for those who had served. It was a memorable tradition but I had no idea that Veteran's Day would be so triggering. It caught me by surprise the first year without Jim and was even more difficult to endure than the first Thanksgiving or Christmas. I believe that it is important to prepare for the holidays and to acknowledge that they may be painful. Decide whether you want to keep the old traditions or change them up and talk to your family members about your grief. Most importantly, look to God's word about how to celebrate.

I find solace in the recognition that God gave His only Son, Jesus, as a sacrifice to make it possible for our loved ones to enjoy His company in heaven. I also find it comforting to concentrate on what God wants for us by looking to His word for guidance. Here are some verses for the holidays:

New Year: Isaiah 43:18–19

"Forget the former things; do not dwell on the past.
See, I am doing a new thing! Now it springs up; do
you not perceive it? I am making a new way in the
wilderness and streams in the wasteland."

Valentine's Day: 1 Corinthians 13:1–3

"If I speak in the tongues of men or angels but do not have
love, I am only a resounding gong or a clanging cymbal.
If I have the gift of prophecy and can fathom all mysteries
and all knowledge, and if I have a faith that can move
mountains, but do not have love, I am nothing. If I give
all I possess to the poor and give over my body to hardship
that I may boast, but do not have love, I gain nothing."

Memorial Day: John 15:13

"Greater love has no one than this: to lay
down one's life for one's friends."

Independence Day: 1 Peter 2:16

"Live as free people, but do not use your freedom
as a cover-up for evil; live as God's slaves."

Labor Day: Colossians 3:23

"Whatever you do, work at it with all your heart, as
working for the Lord, not for human masters."

Thanksgiving: Psalm 136:1

"Give thanks to the Lord for He is good. His love endures forever."

Christmas: 1 John 4:9

"This is how God showed His love among us; He sent His one and only Son into the world that we might live through Him."

Thinking of my mother, husband, and son celebrating the holidays together in heaven frees me to celebrate the holidays on earth. If my children are not available because they are celebrating with their in-laws, I take the initiative to celebrate the holidays with other family members or friends. If they are not available, I work on a project (usually a fun project but when desperate I will even clean out a closet) that provides a distraction or gives me a feeling of accomplishment.

The following devotions, written with love by Naomi, helped us navigate through those special days with our focus on God's word.

Most Memorable Moments
from Holy Week

Safe Strong Place (God)
Naomi

I.

Good morning, dear ones . . .

We have just experienced Holy Week!

Story time:

The Lord died on Good Friday . . . and my dad died on Good Friday!

Because my Lord died and rose from the dead . . . my father lives, just has a different address! (One of my most memorable moments!)

II.

Share a memorable moment from Holy Week this year!

III.

I read this in the "Welcome Book" . . . it is so powerful:

"God is with me . . . In the moment,
That is where I need to be also!
Welcoming what I am feeling . . .
Opening my heart to whatever God might do in the moment . . .
God is loving me into being what He breathed me forth to be!
To accept that is a huge step on my Spiritual Journey!"
(Contempletive Outreach with permission)

IV. Prayer

Father, open our hearts to the memorable moments in our lives that change us into the vessels of service that you ordain, desire, and empower. Bless us as we share, the miracles and the challenges that *you* have accomplished in our lives. Thank you for dying for us . . . and we are so blessed to *know* you rose from the dead and sit on the right hand of God our Father. We love you, amen, and amen.

V.

Therefore, accept all the moments . . . they are gifts to me:

1. Share: your five most memorable moments:

2. Now, (after making a list)

    a. Analyze the list

    b. How many were positive? How many negative?

3. Is there one that you did not dare list? What and why not?

Easter

Mary, Mary, and Mary
Safe Strong Place (God)
Naomi

I.

Good morning, dear friends . . . sisters, really by now!

Jim and I are just back from one and a half days in beautiful Sedona . . . to recharge.

Not only were the mountains glorious . . . *but* . . . there were no boxes to unpack! Glorious.

The afternoon before we left for Sedona, we went to the birthday of Leo, one of our great-grandsons, second birthday party. So precious. Both his parents, Liza and Dathan, are great violinists . . . and his name is Leonid (after a famous Russian violinist . . . Liza came with her family at age two from Russia).

His gift from his grandparents, Beth, and Curt was a real violin.

Then . . . our granddaughter, Kylin, and her husband Eric arrived . . . she was due in two days with their first baby and our first great-granddaughter. When she walked in . . . I expected her to look like she was ready to "pop" . . . instead she looked about three months along. And then, in came Eric carrying a twenty-four-hour-old sweet baby girl, Ezmae Beth, 7 lbs. 11 oz. We were shocked and so thrilled. She had a home birth, and her mom

(Beth) and cousin (Hannah, who is an OB/delivery master's in nursing) assisted the midwife. So precious!

One of the delights of our church is our Sunday school class . . . Community Connections . . . and one of the delights that is new these last many months . . . is that Lynda sits with us . . . and I can reach over and squeeze her hand . . . we laugh, we cry, and continuously learn.

II.

Last Sunday, Ed Hackney was the teacher; he teaches often . . . and shared something so poignant, and "new" to my heart about Easter!

Why did Jesus fold the linen burial cloth after His resurrection? The Gospel of John (20:7) tells us that the napkin, which was placed over the face of Jesus, was not just thrown aside like the other grave clothes.

Mary ran and found Simon Peter and the other disciple, the one whom Jesus loved.

The cloth was "folded" and set aside . . . which, in European culture today, and, most likely in Jewish culture then, was a sign that the guest was not finished but would return . . . would come back again!

Perhaps a tiny thing . . . perhaps *not*!

We *know* that He is coming back again for "the Church" . . . that is us! And . . . It may be soon.

Being Icelandic, I was interested to read that a massive volcanic eruption is expected soon in Iceland, which may be the beginning of many more volcanic eruptions! Sound like end-times?

Hmmm . . . would be nice to see your spouses sooner than later and of course, the risen Lord.

I recommend a book for you to study . . . still not too late. It is an easy read, and it is so special.

There are three Marys at the cross . . . Mary of Bethany, Mary of Nazareth, and Mary Magdalene.

The book is *The Women of Easter* by Liz Curtis Higgs . . . if you get it and read it, let me know . . . *you will* be blessed.

III. Prayer

Father, it is Easter time.

We love knowing what *you* did for us on that Friday on the cross.

We love knowing what *you* did for us on that Easter morning when you conquered death!

And . . . we *love* that Mary Magdalene was first to see you, that the disciples were astonished out of their sadness to receive you.

May we also be like the "women of Easter" and fall at your feet and worship you this holy and precious season . . . Easter.

Amen and amen.

IV. Questions

1. Think about the word *mercy* . . .

> *"But God being rich in mercy, because of His*
> *great love with which He loved us..."*
> *Ephesians 2:4*

2. When have you felt you needed mercy?

3. When have you extended mercy?

4. How is mercy different than grace?

Mother's Day

Safe Strong Place (God)
Naomi

I.

Good morning, dear ones!

There is a special day coming on Sunday . . . Mother's Day.

Not everyone is a mother but all of us have mothers, so this day is important for everyone.

How many grands . . . ?

How many greats . . . ?

We are matriarchs . . . from a matriarch!

Give your mother's maiden name and a characteristic about her that you have cherished and modeled for your downline!

II.

As crucial as our mothers were . . . and hopefully we are to our downline . . . God is *more* important.

Question: Do I have a "kingdom heart"? Or am I stuck in the past?

III.

Quotes that challenged me this week:

> *"Our imagination so magnifies the present, because we are continually thinking about it, and so reduces eternity, because we do not think about it, that we turn eternity into nothing and nothing into eternity, and all this is so strongly rooted within us that all our reason cannot save us from it."*
> *Blasé Pascal*

And, in reality, life is a long series of goodbyes . . . this is why our *hope* in Jesus and eternity with Him is so important.

Also . . . what are we leaving that our children will say, "This is what I remember about my mom . . . my grandmother . . . these are the characteristics that I have tried to model" . . . that will be eternally important.

IV.

So . . . what have you said goodbye to?

What are you looking forward to . . . even more critical for today!

V. Prayer

Father, as we approach Mother's Day, let us rejoice and be thankful for our mothers and all the women who helped shape our lives. Please give your peace and grace to all mothers, especially those who are hurting and struggling. Bless them with your love and allow them to show that love to all they encounter. Amen.

VI. Questions

1. So . . . what have you said goodbye to?

2. What are you looking forward to . . . even more important?

3. If you could wave a magic wand . . . what would you hope to be doing, where were you living, what were you doing in five years? Money is not an option in this dream!

4. Do you have a driving passion? What is it? What can you do about it?

Mountains and Valleys (Mother's Day)

Safe Strong Place (God)
Naomi

I.

Good morning, precious mothers/aunts/friends of little ones/ mothers to big ones . . . all of you.

We were with friends for church and brunch, then our son and daughter-in-law came over with lovely flowers and a pleasant afternoon coffee visit.

Katherine was sick . . . but managed to send over her fantastic chocolate chip cookies . . . ready to bake for our freezer . . . and wonderful warm sweet bread. Beth was in Mexico. . . sent lovely flowers . . . and then a beautiful card from one of you . . . and the promise of a precious time to celebrate together by another one of you . . . so a very, very dear day!

Your turn to share something you will cherish about Mother's Day!

II.

We are going back to the Gaither Family Fest in Gatlinburg over Memorial Day weekend with family and friends. It will be our thirtieth year doing this. We *love* it! One year we took fifty people with us . . . this year only about sixteen.

One of my favorite hymns, "God on the Mountain," was written by Bill and Gloria Gaiter:

> *For the God on the mountain*
> *Is still God in the valley*
> *When things go wrong*
> *He'll make them right*
> *And the God of the good times*
> *Is still God in the bad times*
> *The God of the day*
> *Is still God in the night*
> . . . .
> *For the God on the mountain*
> *Is still God in the valley*
> *When things go wrong*
> *He'll make them right*
> *And the God of the good times*
> *Is still God in the bad times*
> *The God of the day*
> *Is still God in the night*
> *"God on the Mountain" by Bill and Gloria*
> *Gaither (Zion Lyrics, accessed 8/12/2022)*

III. Prayer

In one sentence, tell us why you are thankful for your mother.

IV. Questions

1. When have you experienced true mountain experiences?
2. When have you experienced true valley experiences?

3. Do you feel you have learned more from mountain or valley experiences?

4. Did your faith stay constant . . . more or less, when in the valley?

5. Have you been open to sharing your mountain and valley experiences with people, or reluctant?

6. What do you think God would have you do in the future?

Thanksgiving

Give Thanks in All Circumstances
Safe Strong Place (God)
Naomi

I.

Good morning, dear friends. It is the time of Thanksgiving!

1 Thessalonians: 5:18 says: "Give thanks in all circumstances for this is the will of God for you in Christ Jesus."

Wow . . . *all* circumstances!

We are home for Thanksgiving!

All our "birth kids" . . . are leaving town and leaving the dogs with us! What is wrong with this picture? We thought they would invite us for Thanksgiving when they grew up! Oh well, I have a precious "daughter of my heart" . . . you may have met her: Kathy Dempsey . . . and friend David . . . and they are coming for Thanksgiving dinner at 6:00.

II.

Quick go-around!

1. Share your Thanksgiving plans.

2. Share something you are really thankful for this past year!

III.

I have been studying 2 Chronicles.

1. Solomon, David's son, was a *great* king (until the end).

2. Rehoboam, Solomon's son, was anything *but* a great king.

3. He had the benefit of his father's inner circle of wise counselors but rejected their advice and went with the advice that agreed with his own opinion . . . terrible decision.

4. Solid inner circle qualities:

   a. Experience . . .

   b. Heart for God . . . Love the Lord, and place His values first.

   c. Objectivity: Seeing and weighing the pros and cons of each issue

   d. Love for people

   e. Complimentary gifts to yours!

   f. Loyalty to your leader.

5. Muse on these characteristics for the questions for today!

IV. Prayer

Father, you gave me a great mother! She constantly encouraged me to choose wonderful friends that I would learn from. And I know that was a foundational truth that led me to marry Jim. Thank you for my mother, amen.

V. Questions

1. My mother always said: "You become like the people you spend time with!" How do you choose people you want to grow to be like?

2. Wow . . . ever thought of that?

3. How many people would you say are in your "inner circle" . . . according to the qualifications above?

4. Are they the same as they were ten years ago? Will they be the same in ten years?

5. Share one or two of these people and why they are in your inner circle.

6. How many would you say *are* in your inner circle?

7. Are your children? Some of them? All of them? None of them?

8. Why or why not to question #6?

9. Why do people drop off, and why are they added?

10. Who are you the most thankful for?

Advent

Jesus Is the Light of the World
A Safe, Strong Place
Naomi

I.

Dear ones, this is such a special time of year . . . perhaps your favorite time of year (at least in the past) . . . perhaps it is the most challenging time of year for you (in this current year) without your spouse . . . perhaps for some of you for the very first time.

For others, it was many years of Christmas ago . . . but still the memories flow . . . and it is hard to be "at the moment," day, month of Christmas.

Therefore . . . perhaps it is time to refocus, reframe, renew this month for God's glory!

Sunday was the first Sunday in Advent . . .

I was not used to Advent being stressed until about fifteen years ago when our church started to have the:

1. Advent wreath . . . symbolizes eternity with Him . . . round.

2. Four candles . . . three purple (stands for hope, and His royalty) and the last to be lit is pink . . . which stands for happiness . . . for joy. . . the Savior has come!

3. A candle is lit (often by a family from the congregation) each Sunday in a sweet ceremony while music is played or scripture read.

II.

Advent brings light into the world . . . He is the light of the world.

1. How can you better portray and be His light . . . His candle in a dark world this session . . . so that the blind may see . . . those groping along the "wall" . . . looking for "the door" you can stand at and bring them to the latch.

2. Example of a person who was able to do that when his heart was breaking is Horatio Spafford, who wrote the hymn "It is Well With My Soul" after losing his four daughters.

"When peace like a river attendeth my way,
when sorrows like sea billows roll;
whatever my lot, thou hast taught me to say,
"It is well, it is well with my soul. "
Refrain (may be sung after final stanza only):
It is well with my soul;
it is well, it is well with my soul.
Though Satan should buffet, though trials should come,
let this blest assurance control:
that Christ has regarded my helpless estate,
and has shed his own blood for my soul. Refrain
My sin oh, the bliss of this glorious thought!
my sin, not in part, but the whole,
is nailed to the cross, and I bear it no more;
praise the Lord, praise the Lord, O my soul! Refrain
O Lord, haste the day when my faith shall be sight,
the clouds be rolled back as a scroll;
the trump shall resound and the Lord shall descend;
even so, it is well with my soul. Refrain

*"It is Well With My Soul," Horatio Spafford. Psalter
Hymnal (Hymnal.org, accessed 8/12/2022)*

Also, another book recommendation: *Becoming Mrs. Lewis* (as in
CS Lewis) by Patti Callahan. Amazing read.

III. Prayer

Oh, Father, may we stand "by the door" of people's hearts as they
open them wide to your heart, to your love, to your life. There
is no greater joy in the world, Lord, thank you for that privilege.
Amen.

IV. Questions

Some of you may have heard me speak about *The Meaning of Gifts*.
Paul Tournier wrote this book years ago, and it prompted my
thinking and speaking about gift-giving.

1. How would you define a gift?

2. Do you have a gift-giving philosophy?

3. Has it changed since your husband died? How? Why?

4. What is one of the most precious gifts you have ever
   received?

5. What is one of the most precious gifts you have ever given?

6. Are you giving more gifts as you get older? Or less? This
   year? Why?

7. Is there more joy in giving or receiving . . . when? Why?

8. How does our faith in Jesus . . . and the true meaning of
   Christmas change our gift-giving philosophy?

9. If you could give anyone . . . or someone . . . any gift . . .
   what would it be?

O Come, O Come, Emmanuel

Safe Strong Place (God)

I.

Good morning, dear ones!

I am in California today for the funeral of a very special speaker friend, Danny Cox, an Ace pilot in the Vietnam War, a fabulous speaker, a member of my Speakers Roundtable, and a very close friend of Robert Schuler and member of his church.

We are also hoping to see Titus and Jess . . . just married in September, to gift them with Christmas dishes . . . as a surprise.

II.

Our circle question this week:

What was the highlight of last week?

III.

Devotional time: Advent Devotional Day 3:

Portions from: "The Gospel of Advent" from a *Christianity Today* insert booklet

Come Lord Jesus!

The Bible ends with the prayer, "Come Lord Jesus."

Echoed in many songs: "O Come, O Come, Emmanuel" and "Come Thou Long Expected Jesus."

Oldest Christian prayer we know (except The Lord's Prayer).

Paul quotes the original Aramaic version, Maranatha, meaning "Our Lord, come"! (1 Corinthians 16:22)

Jesus says, "I am coming soon!" (Revelation 22:12, 2:5, 16; 3:11, 16–15)

Revelation also says it is the prayer of the "spirit and the church"...

The church is the Bride of Christ, and we are to pray:

"Come, Lord Jesus, come."

At Christmas, He comes to us . . .

When we are born again . . . He lives within us . . .

We now wait eagerly for Him *to return again*, because we have met Him already, we know Him!

IV. Prayer

Lord, when we look back to our entrance into the kingdom, it may have been just a childhood prayer. But, oh, we did not know, we did not realize that you had chosen us before the foundations of the world to love you . . . Thank you, thank you, Amen, and Amen.

V. Questions

1. When did you first meet Him?

2. Were you told about Him in your childhood home?

3. When did you invite Him into your life?

4. Do you think much about His return to Earth?

5. Is there someone very close to you who you are praying for their salvation?

Advent and Anna

Safe Strong Place (God)
Naomi

I.

It is Sunday night. I have had church, Sunday school, a National Speakers Association Party, and a high tea party with our daughters, their daughters, and their friends and their daughters. This is our twenty-sixth year to do this . . . all today, Sunday. I am exhausted.

II.

So, I am going to have three of our wonderful gals help me, and as of this time (7:30 Sunday night) . . . they do not know it.

Yesterday morning we had a fantastic event.

Our Women of Momentum committee sponsored a Christmas women's luncheon with Liz Curtis Higgs speaking.

For those who may not know Liz, she has spoken at 1,800 large conferences, written thirty-seven books, and sold over five million copies.

It was an amazing event.

We had 350 women . . . an artisan marketplace before, all to raise money for women to have scholarships to attend Phoenix Seminary.

Judy has been the head of this committee for "three hundred years" . . . and it was her "last event" as chair . . . she moved into an emeritus advisory role. I have been on this committee for many years also.

Liz spoke about one of the "Women of Christmas":

1. Her name is Anna.

2. She had spent her life in the temple, fasting, worshiping, praying in expectation for the promised Messiah to come.

3. You remember that Mary and Joseph took baby Jesus to the temple to be blessed!

4. Anna could not contain herself with joy . . . and became the "first Christian woman speaker," telling all that would hear her that she had seen the Messiah.

5. One of the applications that Liz brought out was the importance of an older woman in the faith, an "Anna," to be in your life, to mentor and bless you.

III. Prayer

Father, we are privileged to be "older" than someone. Older than many . . . and thus we have the privilege, your mandate, to teach them, to love them, to care about them, and not to just focus on our peers, and those we want to spend our selfish time with. Open our eyes and our hearts to mentoring others; thank you, thank you, Amen.

IV. Questions

1. Is there an "Anna" in your life? Tell us about her.

2. Has God revealed something new to you this Advent season? (Moment of conception.)

3. Do you find it easy to talk about your faith? Are you like Anna?

4. If not, why not?

The Sinless Lamb

Safe Strong Place (God)
Naomi

I.

It is Christmas week. The trees are up and decorated, lights are brilliant and lovely, Christmas dishes are "out" of the closet, and gifts are wrapped under the tree.

Why?

When we study the Old Testament, we are astonished at how "unholy" the Jewish people were . . . those descendants of Abraham and Moses, David, Solomon, and the prophets were so sinful!

Why?

Because they were created with a sinful nature, and they "gave into it" . . . as we do.

Then, there were four hundred years of silence . . . God did not speak through the prophets . . . no Bible per se . . . all hope seemed to be lost.

Until an Angel announced to a fifteen-year-old girl, engaged to a guy . . . she was going to have a baby, and it was the long-awaited Messiah!

Isn't it amazing . . . to really, really, really think about that?

This Messiah was coming to award their *hope* . . . *hope,* of a sinless Lamb, a light in a dark world, a sprout from the "root of Jesse."

The Messiah was coming . . . to a smelly manger in a barn in Bethlehem.

That was the first "home" for the savior of mankind!

Hmmm . . . *home* . . . that is what I want us to focus on today!

Home, home, home . . . then, now, and forever after!

II.

The verse for today is about *home:*

> "At that time, I will gather you; at that time, I will
> bring you home. I will give you honor and praise
> among all the peoples of the earth when I restore your
> fortunes before your very eyes,' says the Lord."
> Zephaniah 3:20

III. Prayer

Father, may we stop and be thankful for the homes that we have lived in, thankful for the influences we have had in those homes. May we continually open our homes now to those who need your love and kind words. May we strengthen the definition of "home" meaning far beyond the stuff of brick and mortar, but the substance that was represented in that smelly stable "home for Jesus' birth" . . . love, angels, peace, joy, worshippers . . . may it be so, Amen.

IV. Questions

1. Share a story about what "home" was like for you as a child.

2. Was there a Christmas "tradition" in your home?

3. What did you strive to do the same or different in the "home" you and your husband formed from the home you were raised in?

4. As life seasons have changed . . . what do you do the same or different now to make your "home"/home?

5. And . . . home for whom? Who do you invite into your "home" at this season of your life to share the Christmas story of His love?

Christmas: Hope for A Ruined Humanity

Safe Strong Place (God)
Naomi

I.

Merry Christmas, dear, dear ones . . .

II.

It is a special week. The year of this writing, I saw the Christmas
Star. Jupiter and Saturn came together and were visible for the
first time in eight hundred years. It sent chills down my back . . .
so bright . . . what must the shepherds have thought?

The only thing missing was the multitude of angels singing
Monday night. But I listened loudly . . . and I think I did hear
them. (OK . . . she is losing it.)

The theologian J.I. Packer, who passed on to eternity earlier this
year, sums it up:

> *"The Christmas message is that there is hope for a ruined
> humanity—hope of pardon, the hope of peace with
> God, the hope of glory—because at the Father's will,*

Jesus Christ became poor and was born in a stable so that thirty years later He might hang on a cross."

The heavenly host proclaimed, "Do not be afraid," and that was one of the things he came to free us from . . . fear . . . concerns, worry, pain . . . even loneliness . . .

This is the Christmas message!

You have been on my heart this whole session, especially those who are newly without your loved one. And also, those who have spent years now at Christmas without your love. But you still have a love of the Christ child!

Also, many of you who have lost other loved ones—a father, a mother, a close friend . . . a sister, a brother!

I lost my brother in January . . . it was so hard. I was privileged to be with him when he died. He was in a coma, but his pain was so great that he would break through the morphine and wince in horrible pain. His daughter, wife, and I were at his bedside, where we had been for two days. His daughter was weeping, "Dad has kept so many people out of pain . . . . now he is in such pain, I can't stand it." I got charismatic . . . raised my hands and pleaded out loud with the Lord to take him out of his pain. We looked down, and he was gone . . . gone. Not dead, gone . . . to be with Jesus. And out of pain. Because Jesus came and died in pain so that we might live eternally with Him.

III.

Then Monday . . . I saw a video . . . I want to share with you . . . it is a song sung by a dear friend of mine . . . Larry Mathis. The title of the song is "Mary, Did You Know?"

Larry also lost his brother just weeks ago . . . and I invited him to visit with us . . . not a planned agenda . . . just a visit, about how loss affects us during the holidays. . . how Christmas is different after loss . . . and maybe some memories of his brother. Share your name, where you are from, and when you lost your spouse . . .

I came across this poem . . . perhaps you have heard it. . . but I want to share it with you as we look forward to Christmas Eve and Christmas Day!

One thing I know is that Jesus is there . . . and He is here also . . . because He is omnipresent . . . isn't that amazing?

IV. Prayer

Oh, Father, Christmas is filled with so much emotion. The power of the Christmas story sometimes gets lost in the holiday fuss and flurry. Forgive us. May we be mindful of those who have lost loved ones, especially at this time of year. There are places empty at tables and voices that are silent yet heard in our hearts. Heal us, Lord, with your merciful love, and fill us with the real joy of your coming to earth for us! Amen.

V. Questions

1. What do you want to happen next year if you had a magic wand?

2. Share how the holidays were for you.

3. Did you have any "alone time"?

4. Do you remember a time that was sweet or sour? God exhorts us repeatedly to remember; remember His blessings and His deliverance from hardships.

5. How did family relate to the loss of your (their) loved one?

New Year: Change

Safe Strong Place (God)
Naomi

I.

Good morning, dear ones. We celebrate a brand-new year!

I have been reading a sweet, small book, *A Time to Selah: God's Prophetic Invitation for You to Step out of Crisis and Enter into His Perfect Peace,* by Lana Vawser.

Excellent excerpt and concepts for our introduction today:

Background:

King David was greatly distressed (we would be too). He had lost two wives, and people spoke of stoning him!

1. He chose . . . not to be bitter . . . but better!

2. He chose to strengthen himself in the Lord . . . he rose above what was going on in his soul . . . his reality!

Jesus has deep compassion for what you are experiencing . . . through the losses in your life, in my life!

I believe He also wants us not to live in sadness and disappointment, bereavement . . . to choose to believe again and live again.

It is a new year . . . a time for new thoughts . . . New ways . . . *change.*

My last year's theme was "Come and See with 20/20 Vision."

That has been powerful.

Sometimes we need to take off our sunglasses (the why's, the but's, and the I can't) to have a loving view of the Son.

The Son who came to help us through, up, and beyond!

A great idea for the new year:

David's choices:

1. David took all patiently and exercised his faith in his God.

2. He encouraged himself in the power and providence of God.

3. He encouraged himself in the promises of God and His faithfulness in keeping them.

4. He did this in view of his covenant relationship with God.

5. He did this in remembrance of God's grace, mercy, and goodness.

> *"And because of his former experiences of it, hoping and believing that God would appear for him in some way, he strengthened himself in the Word of the Lord his God, in Christ the Word of God, and in the power of His might and grace."*
> *Ephesians 6:10; 2 Timothy 2:1*

II. Prayer

Father in heaven, thank you for the new beginnings this new year brings. May we see your plan for us unfold and help us show your love to all that we encounter, even through the sorrow we face as we grieve the loss of our spouse. Shine your light through us and let us desire you above all else. Amen.

III. Questions

1. Challenge to find a theme for 2021 to share next time and why . . .

2. Magic wand . . . what do you want to have happen in 2021?

3. Share how the holidays were for you.

4. Did you have "alone time for you"?

5. Did you have time to remember both the sweet and sour of life? *Remez* means "remembering" in Hebrew. God exhorts over and over for us to "remember" . . . remember His blessings, His deliverance from hardships.

6. How did family relate to the loss of your loved one . . . their loved one?

7. Did you make any New Year's resolutions? Want to share them?

8. What are you most hopeful will happen next year?

9. What are you most hopeful will not happen next year?

Valentine's Day

Safe Strong Place (God)
Naomi
Love Story Time

I.

Happy Valentine's Day . . . oh . . . You are probably saying, "You have got to be kidding, my valentine is gone!"

I would like to differ with you:

1. Your valentine has a different address . . .

2. But . . . don't you love the "buts" in life?

3. Do you remember as a child, you bought a package of valentines at the dime store and wrote them to *all* your friends?

4. It is time to write and send valentines today . . . tear open the package and pull them all out on the table, or is it a card table . . . do you remember those?

5. Start addressing them and signing different things on the back of them.

II. Prayer

To the one we love the most! Father God, light in our darkness, you are first in our hearts. You provided a partner for us who was dear to our hearts but is now with you. Although your plan for him is finished, you are not yet done with us. Please allow us to fulfill the plan you have in our lives and to remember that you are always with us and we are never alone. Amen.

III. Questions

1. Who do you want to send love to today, and why?

2. Think of a favorite teacher, neighbor in the past, a medical worker in your life, a relative, or a friend that died recently and you would like to send to that person, or someone very current.

3. How about Jesus? What would you say to Him on the valentine?

4. And . . . your spouse has moved to heaven . . . what do you want to remind him of . . . what memory, what part of your love story do you want to write to him?

CPSIA information can be obtained
at www.ICGtesting.com
Printed in the USA
BVHW041805161222
654422BV00001B/16